Praise for Pay Check

"Pay Check is a bold and impassioned book, rich in wry humour, thoughtfully argued throughout... highly persuasive... the starting-point for a worthy and necessary discussion about the nature of talent." – *The Economist*

"[Bolchover's] criticisms of the way top pay is handled [is done] crisply and with good use of data. Many of the hand grenades he throws hit their targets. He is withering about the clichéd term talent, which is used to justify excessive pay." – *The Financial Times / Los Angeles Times*

"A great little book." – *Merryn Somerset Webb, Editor, MoneyWeek*

"A must read for anyone interested in the topic." – *Lynda Gratton, Professor of Management Practice, London Business School*

"The answer and the solution [to excessive pay] lies in an excellent book by the business writer David Bolchover called Pay Check." – *Johann Hari, GQ Magazine*

"A useful reminder for remuneration committees to start asking: how much is too much?" – *Management Today*

"Just learn from and enjoy the delicious demolition of corporate executive pay you'll find in these pages." – *Institute for Policy Studies, Washington*

"The book strongly questions the case for multi-million pound City bonuses and pay deals in the face of the financial crisis and recession." – *People Management*

"As David Bolchover points out in his new book, Pay Check, senior executives pay lip service to talent but rarely do anything concrete about it." – *HR Magazine*

PAY CHECK

Are top earners really worth it?

BY DAVID BOLCHOVER

First published 2010 by
Coptic Publishing
Office 408, 10 Great Russell Street,
London WC1B 3BQ

A catalogue record for this book is available from the British Library.

Library of Congress Cataloging-in-Publication Data

Bolchover David, 1966-
Pay Check: Are top earners really worth it?

ISBN 978-0-9558771-2-4

1. Economics, finance, business and management.
2. Society and social sciences.

Printed and bound in Great Britain by Lightning Source

To Janie, Yael and Joe

CONTENTS

CHAPTER 1

The Poison Carrot

"There are 86,400 seconds in a day. Make every one count." So ran an advertising slogan for the global investment bank, Barclays Capital, in 2008.

The company's American chief executive certainly couldn't have been accused of hypocrisy. During the previous year, Robert E Diamond Jnr. had been awarded total remuneration worth approximately $30 million, or $80,000 for every day in the year, $1 for every second. His seconds certainly count. Tick, tock, tick, tock, tick...another five bucks in the Diamond coffers! Not bad for an employee, a thirty-year corporate veteran who has never traded the comfort of company life for the risks of entrepreneurship.

If Mr. Diamond is the jealous type, he would be advised not to read on. In 2006, Ray R. Irani, the chief executive of the Occidental Petroleum Corporation, took home a total of $460 million. That's around $1,250,000 for every day in the year, or $15 for every second. In the time it took Mr. Irani to brush his teeth in the morning, more than $1,000 would have landed in his bank account. Since he left university in 1957, he has been an employee.

Meanwhile, top professional soccer players in England or Spain can earn more in a couple of days than the average worker does in a year.

And all for kicking a piece of leather around a patch of grass!

Are top earners really worth it? And on what grounds should we decide? There are plenty of commentators who tell us that even entering this discussion is a waste of time. Pay is simply an inevitable product of the market, they say, as if that market existed in a vacuum, unaffected by people's opinions.

Robert Peston, the BBC's business editor, once asked the question "Is Bob Diamond worth the £22m, or £420,000 per week, he earned last year (2006)?", before informing us that he had "a simple, atavistic view: you're worth what you're paid. If you think you're worth more, go out into the marketplace and test it."

Really? What precisely is this "marketplace", and does it work properly? Do top earners genuinely make a huge impact on the performance of their organisations? Are they really as irreplaceable as their supporters claim?

In asking these fundamental questions and challenging many received wisdoms, this book aims to drag the debate about high pay away from the traditional, over-familiar ding-dong, with one side harping on about greed and inequality, and the other accusing us of naivety for even daring to question the workings of the market. Pay always gets us talking. But we are not talking about it in the right way.

In this book, I shall look at the highest earners in our society – entrepreneurs, sports stars, celebrities and, most controversially, senior corporate executives and finance workers – and address the question that we are so often told is too silly to ask: Are they really worth it? And if not, why not?

What exactly is a "Market for Pay"?

Testing the Water

Let's resist the powerful temptation to side automatically with one side or the other of the traditional debate, and instead examine

Mr. Peston's proposition. He tells us (and he is far from alone) that if we aren't happy with what we are earning, we could always test our worth in the marketplace.

Fine in theory perhaps, but how does the market for pay actually function? In the case of hundreds of millions of public-sector workers worldwide, pay will reflect the sum allotted by the state for the particular worker's level and role, and that's pretty much the end of the matter. For them, the market barely applies.

In the private sector, Peston's logic has more value. Take the independent businessperson. She certainly knows what it means to test her worth in the marketplace. Indeed, the very notion itself is axiomatic. She sets up a business and exposes that business to the marketplace. People either buy her products or they don't.

The performance of her business is measurable, and it is also inseparable from her personal performance as a business owner. Of course, the scale of the business's ultimate success will also depend on the contribution of other people, but there wouldn't even be a business at all without the owner. It would be difficult to argue that Larry Page and Sergey Brin, the founders of Google, don't deserve their massive wealth.

With most salaried employees in the private sector, Peston's rationale is also generally valid. The vast majority will earn a salary that is similar, give or take a negligible percentage, to what others with identical experience, performing the same functional role, are earning in other companies. If you don't like your salary of $40,000 for being a retail store manager, then go and try to earn $45,000 at another store.

The labour of the retail store manager is regarded by employers as a commodity. He or she may be good at their job, but it is accepted that there will be plenty of adequate replacements out there should the need arise.

Messi Logic

What about the other end of the pay scale? For the "market" to work efficiently and transparently for the highest paid, one needs, with a reasonable degree of accuracy, to be able to measure that person's performance, assess his specific impact on a desired outcome, and demonstrate beyond reasonable doubt that his abilities are sufficiently rare to make him extremely difficult to replace.

Let's take, for example, a top sports star such as Lionel Messi, an Argentinean soccer player widely regarded as one of the best in the most popular and global sport around.

Messi's individual performance and impact are indeed very measurable; not completely measurable, of course, because he has team-mates and a coach who help him, and he might not perform as well in a lesser team with a less able coach. But they are nonetheless measurable to a marked degree.

He scores many goals, he assists others to score, and to any soccer aficionado watching the game (of which there are millions) his superior skill is self-evident. His club, Barcelona, can make a reasonable assumption that they would not win as many trophies, and earn the resulting prize money, without him.

Messi's individual performance and impact as a soccer player are not only very observable; they are also extremely rare. Hundreds of millions of boys in the world play soccer, and many of them dream of World Cup glory. If they had equivalent natural ability to Messi, we can say with some confidence that it probably would have been spotted already. Even poverty is no barrier – many great stars have hailed from the favelas of South America.

So Messi's skills not only exceed those of the vast majority of his peers, but also those of any potential players. His employer, Barcelona, can reasonably conclude that his value has been tested in the market. The club would therefore be ill-advised to lower his salary – on the assumption that there are plenty like him on the streets of Buenos Aires or Manchester – and then tell him to lump it if he doesn't like it.

In short, Messi has talent. If you work in the world of large corporations, you might recognise that word. It is used a lot there, and that in itself makes me suspicious.

The Corporate Problem

Now how would such market mechanisms apply to the chief executives (CEOs) of major public companies? According to the theory, at least, highly-paid CEOs are, like Lionel Messi, immensely talented; indeed, so rare is their talent that should a company balk at their high financial demands, there would be many a rival firm willing to stump up the asking price. And, as a result, the former company, bereft of such brilliant leadership, would suffer.

But let us examine whether these "market" assumptions are indeed provable or even rational. Can the astronomical increase in executive pay that we have witnessed in recent decades really be explained by this market theory?

In the United States, the average CEO earned 42 times the average blue-collar worker's pay in 1980. By 2000, that multiple had increased more than twelve-fold, to 531. To look at the same remarkable trend in a different way, the average total compensation paid by US public companies to their top five senior executives increased from 5 per cent of profits in the period 1993 to 1995 to around 10 per cent in the period 2001 to 2003. In other words, huge sums of money are being diverted from the owners of the company, and perhaps from other employees, to the senior executive team.

Let's remember, the senior executive is unlikely to be the founder of the company or its majority shareholder. He will be the captain of the ship but he won't have bought the business or built it from scratch. The business would still have existed had he never been born.

Nor can his impact be measured in the same way as Messi's. In a large public company, there will be tens of thousands of employees. The contribution of any one employee will be much more difficult to pinpoint in such a vast organisation than in a soccer team of eleven players.

One can of course say that a company has improved its performance under the leadership of a chief executive. But, as I shall show in the course of this book, it takes a giant leap of faith to attribute a company's success to the abilities of a single individual or team at the top. The company may have performed well despite its leadership, not because of it.

Many more additional factors, other than the alleged abilities of the CEO and his entourage, can be entered into the mix to explain corporate performance. To name but three: a buoyant economy is likely to help the company by increasing demand for its products, or contributing to a rise in its stock price. Lack of competition within its industry may make it easier to make profits. Or perhaps the company has an excellent group of inspiring middle managers who have been the key determinant of success, while the top executives may be little more than front men.

Indeed, those who seek to defend high executive pay would find it difficult to deny there's a degree of arbitrariness in their position. But maybe they feel that they don't need to. If there's just a mere possibility that senior executives could have a decisive impact on results, then they might conclude that it is better to be safe than sorry, and just pay the "going rate".

Stab in the Dark

Let's accept, for the sake of argument, that senior executives might feasibly have a major influence on company performance. To award them extremely high pay, we would also need to prove that their ability to exert this possible influence is extremely rare. As every economics student knows, when a product (or employee) is in short supply, its price (or wage) must increase. Are senior executives paid so well because they have such rare ability?

Again, at best, this is extremely difficult to prove, or even state with any degree of confidence. If the top man can boast a track record of having led other profitable companies, this might arguably strengthen his case. But, as we have seen, such success might have owed extremely little to his alleged abilities.

What's more, most senior executives appointed have no such track records anyway. In 2007, 68 per cent of newly named CEOs at the world's 500 largest companies were hired from inside the company. Some more, no doubt, had been appointed as chief executives immediately after being recruited from below the top level in other companies. Selection is therefore made, in this majority of cases, on potential, not past performance in a similar role.

What then would be the attributes of an individual who has the potential to be an effective chief executive? Proven performance at a lower level, perhaps? But any large company will have many managers who can claim this and, besides, it is far from easy to determine the contribution of any one individual to departmental or regional success, let alone company-wide success.

The chief executive position is also arguably a very different role from a more junior manager, perhaps requiring very different skills. Companies themselves certainly appear to believe that the abilities required at the top level are far rarer. If they didn't, they surely wouldn't feel the need to pay the chief executive so much more.

In the absence of a wholly relevant career history, certain personality characteristics are likely to be sought – virtues such as intelligence, diplomacy, affability, credibility, persuasiveness, presence, insight, rigour and energy. While these are all commendable, I can honestly say that several of my own personal acquaintances and business contacts possess all of these characteristics in abundance.

Indeed, it could well be the case that the pool of potentially excellent chief executives, with impressive-looking experience below the top level, is really quite substantial. Messi may be replaceable by only a tiny few; to say the same about a chief executive stretches credulity.

We are told to bow to the decisions of the marketplace. But that marketplace for pay, in the very high-profile and influential case of chief executives, is based on what seems, on further analysis, to be mere conjecture, and very flimsy conjecture at that.

Exploiting the Fog

So let me offer a very different explanation for high pay at the top of the corporate world – an explanation that I shall develop throughout the course of this book.

Chief executives, senior executives, high-flyers who aspire to be senior executives, pay consultants who are hired by senior executives, business school academics and management consultants who sell their services to senior executives, and representatives from institutional shareholders whose executives are often themselves extremely well-paid, have neatly sidestepped, or even made use of, the difficulties inherent in identifying the true value of individual performance within very large corporations, in order to further their own financial agenda.

Vested interests have constructed and subsequently jealously guarded an entire ideology of "talent", a self-serving distortion of the real meaning of the word. This ideology holds, without anywhere near sufficient evidence, that the individual value of senior executives is extremely precious.

Their case has not been robustly challenged, partly because it is just as difficult to counter the ideology as it should be to construct it in the first place. The originators and the upholders of the talent ideology ignored the near-impossibility of measuring individual contribution in large corporations, and then hoped that the rest of us would be intimidated by this near-impossibility into remaining silent.

They have used their positions of influence and status to propagate a self-interested doctrine, assuming, correctly, that we would simply defer to our betters even if we sensed, deep down, there was something rotten going on.

Meanwhile, those inside the company are either too fearful or respectful of their superiors in the hierarchy to question it; or they themselves have a vested interest in a system that might eventually promote them, or already rewards them, albeit at a lower level, for contributing rather less than their salary might suggest.

The pay "marketplace" that commentators refer to is, in reality, based on entirely subjective assessments which render it corruptible. In the case of senior corporate executives (and many relatively junior staff in the financial sector), such corruption is now prevalent. For society as a whole, the consequences of this are numerous and profound.

Why is excessive pay a problem?

Beyond Envy

If irrationally high pay barely affected anyone beyond the recipients and those who profit from their wealth, then the whole subject might not be worthy of protracted discussion. Attacking it might then merely appear to be a result of envy, a negative and harmful emotion that we should not pander to.

In the traditional battleground, one side of the debate has maintained that extremely high pay stems from pure greed, and causes great harm to society by promoting inequality and social division. Their opponents generally counter that such views are motivated by envy, that fostering individual excellence often requires financial incentives which lead to inequality, and that those who constantly bemoan greed would rather extinguish inequality than promote excellence.

We have been trapped in this intellectual stalemate for too long. It is time to reject both sides of the customary argument, and move the debate forward.

On the one hand, the accusation of greed levelled at high earners is undeserved and hypocritical. Few would turn down the opportunity to become rich if it was offered to them. Inequality should not in itself concern us: it can galvanise those with rare and valuable ability to make the most of their own potential and create wealth for the rest of society.

On the other hand, those who wholeheartedly believe in the benefits of a free market have too often ignored problems with very high pay that damage the system that they themselves support. They tend to take the view that all legally obtained wealth and high pay are fine, an ultimately self-destructive position. The fact that some people become extremely rich is indeed very healthy, but only provided that they do so for the right reasons.

They say that it is pure envy that drives criticism of high pay. However, most people currently possess a sound sense of when high pay or wealth is deserved, at least as far as the business world is concerned. They might not have thought through, as this book attempts to do, why they think like they do, but they think it nonetheless. And envy doesn't have much to do with it.

Few, outside a marginal fringe that completely rejects the system of free market enterprise, would dispute the claim of a successful self-made entrepreneur to the money she has earned. With her own ingenuity and hard work, she has created wealth and jobs galore, not to mention products that people want to buy.

People are unlikely to think the same way about Richard Fuld, the former chairman and chief executive of Lehman Brothers, who earned $40.5 million in 2006 and $34 million in 2007 (around $100,000 a day), before the company that employed him went bust in 2008. In fact, they are unlikely to think the same way even about a similarly paid corporate leader who has presided over sustained success.

Opinion polls confirm this distinction in public attitudes towards entrepreneurial wealth on the one hand, and executive wealth on the other. According to a Financial Times/Harris poll of November 2007, most people feel that successful entrepreneurs "should be allowed to keep a substantial share of the wealth they create". Almost two thirds in the United States, as well as majorities in UK, Germany and Italy, and just under one half in France, agree with this statement.

But according to another Financial Times/Harris poll, this time in April 2009, the vast majority of people agree that "business leaders are generally paid too much". Around 80 per cent of respondents in the United States, UK, Germany, France and Spain supported this statement, with little variation between the countries.

Many people will, of course, envy the lifestyle of a top CEO or a successful entrepreneur. But in approving of the latter while being sceptical of the former, we can conclude that ordinary folk manage to prevent any feelings of envy from interfering with their judgment about the merits of high pay.

Corrupting the System

This aside about envy is included here for two reasons. First, it seeks to pre-empt the lazy dismissal of any attempt to decide whether high pay is deserved as the mere consequence of envy. Second, we must understand the current distinction in people's minds before we can move on to the first in the long list of the negative consequences of irrationally high pay.

I have argued that vested interests have used the opaqueness of large corporate life to promote a self-interested ideology. They have benefited from our unwillingness or inability to confront their claims for inflated pay. This failure to tackle the prevailing view has led to a dangerous corruption of the relationship between pay and value.

The word "dangerous" is not used lightly here. The risk of this corruption is potentially systemic. Opinion polls might demonstrate that people currently make a distinction between deserved entrepreneurial rewards and undeserved executive pay. However, in times of economic hardship, people can easily fall prey to the populism that pays no heed to subtle distinctions. As they suffer, they see others sitting on an undeserved fortune, making them susceptible to appeals for punitive taxation, or even mass nationalisation.

Angry and confused, a deeply unpleasant and potentially volatile emotional combination, and feeling like the victims of an elaborate swindle, people might feasibly be tempted to throw out the free market baby with the dirty bathwater of excessive pay. Popular resentment may be difficult to contain.

There is, also, a second systemic risk posed by irrationally high pay that became apparent during the international banking crisis of 2008. Employees in the investment banking industry had used the same "talent" argument to award themselves massive bonuses. If they brought in $100 million of revenue into the company, they ought to receive, say, $10 million of that for themselves. After all, who else but the "talented" could bring in so much money?

Many of the rest of us felt somehow uncomfortable with this situation, but we obeyed the established doctrine and let it go. Let the market decide! But when it emerged that these huge individual financial rewards were based not upon rare talent, but rather the pursuit of highly risky investing strategies, it was not the bankers who were punished. Rather, it was the taxpayer who had to rescue the crumbling financial system on which we all depend.

Meanwhile, the more successful bankers happily pocketed their winnings. In the words of the self-made billionaire investor Warren Buffett: "Too many people have walked away from the troubles they have created for society, not just for their own institution, and they have walked away rich."

The realisation of the second systemic risk, individuals pursuing strategies that endanger us all, also aggravates the first systemic risk, the possibility that anger and confusion during straitened economic times will make people vulnerable to authoritarian ideas.

Not only do people see others sitting on undeserved wealth while they endure hardship, they also feel that they are enduring hardship precisely because others took risks to obtain this undeserved wealth. Their subsequent hurry to avenge the perpetrators is likely to make high taxation for top earners more attractive, penalising real entrepreneurs and handicapping business growth.

Risk Deterrence

The damaging repercussions do not stop there. Unchecked rewards at the top of the corporate world, and throughout the financial sector, will inevitably divert a significant number of people away from entrepreneurship, a vital source of energy, competition, ingenuity and growth in our society, and allow them to dream of getting either rich, or very comfortable, as cushioned employees in large companies.

Of course, some people might be born entrepreneurs. Somehow one can't imagine Steve Jobs or Richard Branson dutifully sitting in an office cubicle from Monday to Friday, and picking up a pay cheque. Others show no aptitude or interest in setting up alone.

But a great number are neither born employees nor born entrepreneurs. The ambitious and money-minded among them have a choice. Try to go it alone, knowing that you will get no guaranteed salary and are likely, statistically, to fail anyway. Or try to work your way up a massive corporation, attaining gratifying pay increments along the way, with a potentially massive risk-free pot of gold at the top. Many spend their whole careers weighing up the two alternatives. The former course might seem more romantic, but the latter course is difficult to resist.

A healthy free market system should encourage people to take risks in order to strive for great individual wealth. When people set up a business, it is often because they believe they can offer something different and original that can attract customers and make them large sums of money. If they didn't have such an idea, they perhaps wouldn't take the risk. Many individual start-up businesses might fail, but the general pursuit of wealth through business risk progresses society and the economy by encouraging innovation.

A system that offers ample opportunity for risk-free wealth (to anyone apart from those with very rare, measurable and commercially useful talent) stunts this originality and therefore hinders progress. It encourages people to take up jobs which can be done by many others rather than use all their wits and imagination to create something new and valuable.

Companies might of course argue that the entrepreneurial strength of the wider society is not their concern. Indeed, they might feel the need to offer the pot of gold incentive to stop ambitious and able staff setting up on their own (exploiting the expensive training handed to them by their employer), and encourage them instead to devote themselves to the corporate world.

Office Politics

In the early 1980s, two American economists, Edward Lazear and Sherwin Rosen, developed a related line of thinking. They argued that executives' pay often far exceeded their value, but that the award of such undeserved pay could still be efficient from the company's standpoint.

In their view, the great prize of earning huge wages was the most effective way of inducing great effort from those at the grass roots of the company who hoped that they would one day be beneficiaries of executive pay. In other words, the incentive of high executive pay was good for companies, and presumably, therefore, for the wider society which benefited from companies' increased productivity. They called this idea "tournament" theory.

From the perspective of the companies themselves, according to this logic, high executive pay could be said to have two potentially positive indirect consequences – it helps to retain the right people throughout the organisation and encourages them to work hard. But although that sounds good in theory, the immeasurability of individual performance in large companies, and its offspring, corporate culture, make such reasoning highly dubious in practice.

As individual value is so difficult to measure, other criteria – alliance formation, patronage, self-promotion, superficial perception and sycophancy – can often act as the agents of career success. The net result is a great number of ambitious and able people spending their working lives jockeying for the ideal position from which to chase the pot of gold, rather than building new businesses for the benefit of the consumer and the economy.

Some might say that very few people can realistically aspire to the relatively small number of top positions in the corporate world and, as a consequence, the rewards associated with these positions only create a very weak disincentive to entrepreneurship.

However, a disproportionately high number of ambitious and able people will feel they can get near to the top. High senior executive pay will therefore act as a stronger deterrent to entrepreneurship for those arguably more likely to succeed as entrepreneurs.

Moreover, in the finance sector, you do not need to reach the top to become extremely wealthy. For example, in the City of London alone, it was estimated that 4,200 workers received bonuses in excess of £1 million ($1.7 million) in 2007.

Banks that were bailed out by government money during the 2008 crisis were quick to pay million-dollar bonuses to their staff during the very same year. For example, JP Morgan Chase paid out 1,626 bonuses in excess of $1 million and Goldman Sachs paid out 753. With bad years like that, who needs good ones?

Low Expectations

Aside from its economic costs, excessive pay serves to limit human potential. Individuals are rendered more likely to spend their lives engaged in repetitive, unchallenging jobs in soulless offices rather than stretching themselves, perpetually racking their brains about how to get ahead of the competition and make money. How many great ideas never see the light of day, how much energy is wasted, how much creative spark is extinguished in this way?

Worse, the myth of rare talent that justifies executive pay also implies that the vast majority of people are untalented, and because of this implicit label, makes it much less likely that they will achieve their real potential. As the academic Jeffrey Pfeffer put it: "Labelling only a few as stars will cause the majority to perform way below their potential. The self-fulfilling prophecy is one of the oldest and most established principles for understanding organisational behaviour. Simply put, the self-fulfilling prophecy holds that high expectations increase performance and low expectations will decrease performance."

The low expectations of others damage self-confidence and increase anxiety, thus tending to stifle achievement. These same low expectations also make hard work seem pointless. If you believe that you're mediocre, then why push yourself?

Unjustified high pay also cements a very damaging entitlement culture within modern society, offering the vision of relatively effortless wealth, success or security. Famous up-from-the-bootstraps entrepreneurs set a fine example to young people. Their life stories affirm the existence of great opportunities, but remind us that in order to seize them, you need originality and the persistence and self-belief to withstand the inevitable dark periods on the road to realising the dream.

The enormous publicity surrounding executive and finance sector pay in recent years negates this message, instead signaling to young people that wealth simply gets given to those who manoeuvre themselves into the right place at the right time. A dynamic society needs people to aspire to wealth through their inventiveness and conscientiousness, not through their wiliness in climbing the greasy corporate pole.

More Hands in Pockets

All the time, the money that finances the high salaries paid in public-listed companies comes largely from individuals and from institutional shareholders such as pension funds and investment trusts – in other words, from the hard-earned savings of ordinary citizens.

According to one estimate, at least 310 million people in 59 countries own stock directly, and at least 503 million individuals in 64 countries own stock indirectly through pension fund holdings. Money that undeservedly goes into the deep pockets of a senior executive has been unfairly taken from the shallow pockets of a great many average Joes throughout the world. Companies that fail or run into trouble because highly-paid employees were prioritising their own personal financial interests cost their shareholders (you and me) vast sums of money.

It's not just the pay of the man at the top that we have to worry about. There are management tiers below the top whose pay will inevitably track the upward trajectory of the pay awarded to the CEO. We can't prove this conclusively, because public companies currently only have to reveal directors' salaries. But we can get a fair idea of what is happening.

For example, Jeffrey Immelt, the chairman and chief executive of General Electric, told CNBC in January 2007 that his pay should have a reasonable relationship with his top 20 reports in GE, and remarked that it would be "weird" if his earnings were 14 to 15 times that of the vice-chairman. Immelt earned $14.2 million during that same year.

Furthermore, those seeking to fill management jobs in the state sector, perhaps in local government or in a nationalised health system, may start to believe that they have to compete with executive salaries in the private sector in order to attract the best "talent".

In the UK, a few years of unobtrusive and inoffensive service as a head of a local government authority can set a person up for life. In 2007-2008, ten chief executives of local councils earned total annual remuneration of at least £200,000 ($340,000). European commissioners, members of the executive branch of the European Union, are paid €217,280, a similar figure. The average Joe forks out again, this time through his tax bill.

Pay Matters

The severity of the 2008 banking crisis, and the ensuing global recession, has triggered a fundamental rethink about our economic system. Any attempt to renew that system without actively confronting the question of high pay will be wholly inadequate and ultimately futile.

But the debate on this issue has so far failed to go deep enough, and its terms must be fundamentally shifted if real progress is to be made. Excessive pay rests on false assumptions about talent and the nature of the modern-day workplace. Governments, regulators and experts may recommend and implement complex solutions to tackle excessive pay, but the underlying false assumptions themselves remain very much intact. We urgently need to get to the root of the problem, and expose these received wisdoms for what they are.

This book will challenge the self-interest, resignation and complacency that sustain the status quo and its pernicious effects. The market for pay is not set in stone. It is based on opinions, often self-serving ones, and those opinions can and must be examined afresh.

CHAPTER 2

The Talent Ideology

In the closing months of 2008, the insurer AIG and the financial services company Citigroup were rescued from bankruptcy by US federal bailout money amounting to a combined total of $215 billion, approximately the total annual Gross Domestic Product of Hong Kong or Portugal. By March 2009, less than six months later, their respective chief executives had railed against any attempted government interference in their pay awards to senior executives.

Edward Liddy, the then AIG chief executive, wrote a letter to the US Treasury Secretary, Tim Geithner. The letter argued that the company "cannot attract and retain the best and brightest talent to lead and staff the AIG businesses... if employees believe that their compensation is subject to continued and arbitrary adjustment by the US Treasury."

In the same week, Vikram Pandit, the Citigroup chief executive, argued that any punitive taxation of his company's high earners would be counterproductive. In a memo to employees, he wrote: "The work we have all done to try to stabilize the financial system and to get the economy moving again would be significantly set back if we lose our talented people because Congress imposes a special tax on employees." Pandit's total compensation was itself estimated at more than $38 million in 2008, the very year American taxpayers saved the company that employed him to run it.

We can draw two, related, conclusions here. First, these comments surely dispel any lingering naïve view that the 2008 banking crisis will in some way discourage high pay in the financial sector. If the leaders of banks recently resuscitated by the government are insisting that their employees need to be rewarded with high net pay, then you can bet your bottom dollar that the industry as a whole will be defending extremely high pay during future bull markets. Indeed, as we shall see later, bumper bonuses were already returning to certain parts of the financial sector during 2009.

Second, we see very clearly how those who defend high pay attempt to justify it. It is "talented" employees, Liddy and Pandit both say, who must be rewarded without undue constraints. "Talent" implies rarity. A rare and commercially valuable commodity commands a high price.

When the management of companies kept alive by government assistance claim to know what "talent" is, we get some sense of how resilient and entrenched the talent ideology has become within the corporate world. It was one thing bandying "talent" about as justification for high pay when companies were making huge profits during a bull market period. But to maintain an identical argument when the same companies are on the floor betrays an unyielding determination.

Defence of high pay in the financial sector is not going away in a hurry, and nor, it appears, is its ideological foundation, "talent". The two go hand in hand. To win the argument against very high corporate pay, and prevent all the damage it causes, one first has to dismantle the talent ideology that underpins it.

Knowledge and Fear

An ideology is the body of ideas that guides an individual, a culture or a group of people. The specific ideology of talent has been espoused by the modern knowledge worker, and in particular, the high-flying knowledge worker.

Peter Drucker, the eminent management writer, was the first to coin the term "knowledge worker" in 1959, as the end of the industrial era was becoming more apparent. Indeed, the knowledge worker, who earns a living through developing or using knowledge, is very much an inhabitant of the post-industrial era.

Although many manual workers will use specialised knowledge to perform their job, the term is now generally understood to mean a white-collar office worker. According to one estimate, some 48 million of the 137 million workers in the United States alone can be classified as knowledge workers. Certainly, these knowledge workers will form the great majority of those earning high pay as employees.

Unlike factory workers and manual tradesmen, knowledge workers are usually unable to demonstrate the physical results of their labour. A factory worker can point to the number of widgets in his tray at the end of the day, but a human resources executive or public relations consultant can only report a subjective view of progress on projects with often ill-defined ends.

Moreover, the commercial usefulness of these projects tends to be very difficult to measure. How do you gauge the impact of a brand promotion campaign on profitability? Any change in profitability might arguably have been caused by any number of factors, either within the company, or in the broader economy, or among potential customers.

Then there is the perennial problem of measurability of individual performance. Even when the output and its commercial usefulness are measurable, such as in a sales department, modern knowledge workers often operate in such large groups that it becomes difficult to identify precisely who was responsible for that measurable output.

If, say, PricewaterhouseCoopers, the largest accounting firm in the world by revenue in 2008, wins the General Electric corporate account, which one of their 155,683 employees is most responsible for that success, who is somewhat responsible, and who is a little bit responsible? For the vast majority of knowledge workers, clear measurability is elusive.

Once one understands this reality, the language and behaviour of the large modern-day office become much simpler to interpret. This lack of measurability presents, at one and the same time, a threat and an opportunity. It creates a deep-seated sense of insecurity on the one hand. And, on the other hand, it allows individuals to win the race up the career ladder not through measurable performance, but by looking and speaking the part, by merely appearing to be able and useful.

While measurability of performance is often very low, the stakes are very high. The knowledge worker's ability to sustain an often expensive lifestyle, or simply put food on the family's table and provide for a decent pension, depends largely on how others view both the commercial value of their knowledge and their ability to use that knowledge. What therefore determines career success, and the resulting social status and financial security, is vague, intangible and discretionary.

With the growth of available information through the expansion of the internet over the last decade, knowledge workers' sense of vulnerability will have heightened immeasurably. What sets them apart from those outside their industry or function is their specific knowledge. Now outsiders can develop a reasonably sophisticated understanding of insiders' everyday activities even through a disciplined and far-reaching online search.

The intimidating mystique of many jobs has been significantly eroded, raising chances of an outsider raid on insider territory. Democratization, a leveling of the playing field, and disintermediation, the removal of unnecessary middlemen, are recent forces that continue to impinge on the world of work, generating the vision of opportunity for hungry outsiders, but also the spectre of increased competition.

Living through broader events and cycles in society at large will no doubt have further exacerbated this feeling of insecurity. Economic downturns, and large-scale redundancies, will be recalled by everyone over a certain age, coincidentally often those with the most financial responsibility to provide for young children and/or elderly parents. Any further experience of recession reinforces that vulnerability. The need to safeguard one's livelihood, to protect it from competition, is intense and overwhelming.

It is within this context of profound fear (and the accompanying opportunity presented by the lack of measurability) that we have witnessed the proliferation of the talent ideology, welcomed enthusiastically as a means to soothe insecurity, elevate self-image, embed position, erect barriers to entry and raise pay.

Fervent Embrace

Although its central tenets had been circulating for some time, the talent ideology was formally set out in a 1998 article, written by five McKinsey consultants. The article, entitled "The War for Talent", appeared to make four points:

A small minority of talented employees have a highly disproportionate impact on company performance; the demands of an increasingly complex global economy would require exceptional leaders with a rare combination of singular attributes; demographic decline would make the search for these extremely effective employees even more challenging; as a result of these factors, companies would contest an ever-intensifying "war for talent" with their competitors.

These arguments became oft-pronounced orthodoxies in the corporate world. Highly paid Global Talent Directors were appointed; conferences to debate the talent issue became fashionable; independent talent consultants swarmed around human resources departments; an entire industry was created. The word "talented", in the main previously reserved for great sports stars, entrepreneurs and artists, became a fixture of the office lexicon.

But a glance at the content of the McKinsey article immediately arouses misgivings in the curious reader. The authors' very definition of talent, the ultimate foundation stone of what was to become a ubiquitous ideology, provides us with little more than a shining example of humourously incomprehensible jargon: "A more complex economy demands more sophisticated talent with global acumen, multicultural fluency, technological literacy, entrepreneurial skills and the ability to manage increasingly delayered, disaggregated organisations."

These are empty words; nobody can honestly claim, with any precision, to know what they mean. However, the ideology did not attain such popularity because of its sharp insight, but because it promoted the interests of the successful but vulnerable incumbents of highly-paid knowledge jobs.

McKinsey, a management consulting firm with a powerful brand associated with innovative ideas, was the ideal author for the article, bestowing its contents with significant credibility. "Making sure top performers' compensation is considerably higher than that of their average colleagues", the article proclaimed, "is a relatively straightforward way to keep the exit price high and raise barriers to poaching." For senior executives and high-flying workers in the financial sector (often, incidentally, McKinsey clients themselves), this was manna from heaven.

Companies subsequently proclaimed ad nauseam that "talent" was a strategic priority not only because they may have believed in some of the assumptions of the ideology, but because doing so rendered it inevitable that those already in positions of influence within the companies (and those who aspired to these positions) would be classified among the endangered species of the talented. A company that repeatedly talked about the importance of talent could only have talented people at the top, couldn't it?

The language used in the McKinsey article and in others' countless follow-up articles is usefully meaningless; it is so devoid of clear meaning that it cannot threaten anyone. Nobody can say "you shouldn't be in your position, we need someone who is more comfortable dealing with disaggregation instead, and you simply don't cut it in a delayered environment". But loudly and consistently hailing the broad concept signals a forward-thinking company with a leadership that is already talented enough to value talent, and therefore worthy of veneration and ever greater compensation, lest their like are never found again.

Muddle Multiplied

The original McKinsey definition of "talent" may be unclear, but the puzzle becomes still more complex when we look at how the word is used. Perhaps the only sense we can glean from the McKinsey definition is that it seems to refer to the cream of the workforce. We don't really know what they mean by the cream, but it is certainly the cream they are talking about. What makes the talent debate appear even more of a futile charade is that many people define talent to be pretty much everyone, the mass of the employee population.

Here are a series of quotes, plucked randomly from interviews and company pronouncements. "Dow Jones is a formidable organisation packed with talented people," says Les Hinton, the company's chief executive. "Our company is full of talented people who we continually develop and enable to reach their highest potential," claims Jonathan Ferrar, Director of Human Resources, IBM (EMEA). "Britain today is full of talented people," avers Stuart Rose, chief executive of Marks and Spencer. "The kind of results we've achieved would not be possible without great effort from the very talented people throughout our organization," opined Sandy Weill in 2002, then chief executive of Citigroup, presumably about a similar collection of "very talented people" who were to come close to destroying their company six years later.

Not only do we not know what constitutes membership of the talented cream, but much of the business world is telling us that to be a "talented person", you do not need to possess an elite ability at all. This person is, to all intents and purposes, just a living, breathing human being. Indeed, in much corporate communication, "talent" now simply means staff.

This line of thinking seems to be a concession to the modern popular consensus, which holds that everyone is "special", and nobody is just ordinary. Executives do not live in a vacuum, and are as liable to express the platitudes prevalent in the surrounding society as anyone else, whether they genuinely believe them or not, at no cost to themselves.

They are also going out of their way to be nice to their fellow employees and compatriots with these comments, hoping, perhaps, that the recipients of their compliments will think more highly of them, or even work harder, in return. We might also add that this supremely broad definition, just as the opaque McKinsey definition, is far too unspecific and meaningless to carry a threat to those at the top.

But what this "everyone is talented" cliché shows above all is that the concept of "talent" is supremely malleable. An unofficial carte blanche allows its meaning to be massaged according to the whims of the speaker, whatever they may be. That whim may be the desire to be liked. It may be the desire to conform. It may be the desire to engender motivation. And what is the foremost work-related desire of the corporate high-flyer? It is to preserve and further their position, and raise their pay. This is the primary utility of a thoroughly versatile word. "Talent" is all things to all men, but to a certain proportion of those men (and they almost always are men), it is a ticket to riches.

Good in Theory?

Notwithstanding this stark contradiction in the corporate world's use of the word "talent", the intellectual basis for very high pay must ultimately rest on the idea that the ability to perform certain jobs is extremely scarce, as the talent ideology holds. Let's ignore for a while my argument that high-flyers have exploited this thinking for their own benefit. If that were indeed true, it doesn't necessarily mean that the ideology itself is fundamentally misguided. It might have been a great theory, subsequently abused, that needs to be applied in a less partisan way.

Let us recap on my own understanding of the key components

of the talent ideology, as originally articulated by McKinsey and subsequently supported by many others. They were: A small minority of talented employees have a highly disproportionate impact on company performance; the demands of an increasingly complex global economy would require exceptionally sophisticated leaders with a rare combination of singular attributes; demographic decline would make the search for these extremely effective employees even more challenging; as a result of these factors, companies would contest an ever-intensifying "war for talent" with their competitors.

The final point is clearly dependent on the first three, so let's look at the others one by one, and see if they stand up. First, we need to examine the article's assertion that "superior talent will be tomorrow's source of competitive advantage."

The McKinsey authors, as we have seen, do not provide a satisfactory definition of "talent", let alone "superior talent", which presumably means something similar. So what might be the most common interpretations of the word? I would suggest that there are two – a high level of mental ability, and a high level of proven performance.

Brain Benefit

Will a high level of mental ability be "tomorrow's source of competitive advantage"? Many companies appear to think so, actively seeking the graduates who have achieved the highest marks at the most prestigious universities and business schools, and paying them a premium for this educational achievement. The average 2009 salary for an MBA graduate from University of Pennsylvania, Wharton was around $170,000, but for an MBA graduate from University of South Carolina's Moore School of Business, it was just over half that level, at around $90,000. Wharton was top of the 2009 global rankings for MBA courses, published annually by the Financial Times.

If you are aspiring to be a professor in Nuclear Physics, then clearly a rare level of intellectual prowess is necessary. In business, too, there are certain jobs where it will, without doubt, make an individual more valuable. A lawyer engaged in an arcane facet of the law, by way of example, or a mathematician developing breakthrough ideas in actuarial work. But for the vast majority of even the most senior and highly-paid jobs in the corporate world, the argument that a high level of intellectual ability is required, or even desirable, is open to question.

Enron was one company that interpreted McKinsey's extremely vague definition of talent to mean a very advanced level of education at a highly prestigious institution. As McKinsey authors explained in their book "War for Talent" (a follow-up to the infamous article), Jeff Skilling, then chief executive of Enron, "decided to bring in a steady stream of the very best college and MBA graduates he could find to stock the company with talent."

In a 2002 essay in the New Yorker, the writer Malcolm Gladwell offered reasons why Enron's recruitment strategy was founded on erroneous principles, and might well have led to its collapse in 2001. First, he refers to research that plays down the influence of academic intelligence on job performance. IQ does have some positive bearing on workplace success (most probably due to the fact that many companies value, perhaps wrongly, the academic success that often derives from high IQ), but many studies have concluded that emotional development, including such attributes as resilience, sensitivity and self-awareness, matters significantly more.

Second, he contends that Enron's "assumption that an organization's intelligence is simply a function of the intelligence of its employees" is fundamentally faulty, maintaining that more prosaic factors, such as efficient company-wide organisation and execution, are more conducive to high corporate performance than a collection of brainy people. Gladwell suggests that this preoccupation with recruiting "stars", and then bending over backwards to keep them happy, diverted necessary attention away from Enron's internal systems, and most importantly, its customers.

Certainly, even more recently than the Enron debacle, the fact that Lehman Brothers, Bear Stearns and other financial institutions recruited their people predominantly from top universities and business schools did not stop them going bankrupt or having to be rescued.

One could argue, too, that a high level of intellectual ability might potentially exert a negative influence on individual job performance, that "superior talent" not only spawns little if any advantage, but actually could be a source of competitive disadvantage.

The majority of even apparently high-powered jobs require persistent application, personal organisation and a high tolerance of the humdrum, the constant repetition of similar tasks. A highly active mind could therefore be a drawback. Arguably, it might be more likely to rebel against dull routine and thereby become dissatisfied with such work more quickly. What's more, it might be more likely to react against the constant obligation to conform in a large hierarchical organisation, to obey the instructions of others without argument.

Even if companies do conclude after honest and careful deliberation that they need highly active minds suited to business, who says that these people will boast a high level of education? Of the 25 wealthiest self-made entrepreneurs in the UK in 2007, only two had received any type of degree from a higher education institution. Sir James Dyson, famous for his design of the vacuum cleaner, graduated with a degree in Furniture and Design from the Royal College of Art. Sir Terence Matthews, the high-tech entrepreneur, earned a degree in Electronics at the University of Swansea, not generally considered a top-tier academic institution.

Indeed, it might be that the achievement of an impressive degree from a top university lessens ambition. Perhaps those without notable educational achievement are hungrier, less complacent, have more of a point to prove. Perhaps universities and business schools instill a damaging orthodoxy in their students, encouraging them all to follow the same techniques or lines of argument.

This might suppress the originality and independent thinking required for innovation, something all companies could do with. As Dame Anita Roddick, founder of the Body Shop, put it: "The problem with business schools is that they are controlled by, and obsessed with, the status quo. They encourage you deeper into the world as it is. They transform you into a better example of corporate man."

To summarise, high pay rests on the talent ideology, on the notion that the ability to perform certain jobs is scarce. One common interpretation of talent is high educational achievement. The evidence to support the theory that high educational achievement makes one better equipped to perform all but a small minority of commercial jobs is insubstantial and inconclusive. It is merely conjecture and, in my own view, it is opposed by more convincing conjecture.

Even if it were true that highly active minds were a prerequisite for excellent performance, educational achievement provides an unsatisfactory barometer. And if one can't measure what we might call "commercial intelligence" by educational achievement, then how exactly should we measure it? And if we can't measure it, why should we reward it with high pay?

Virtuoso Performance

Those who defend the talent ideology might counter that high educational achievement is rarely in itself a passport to extremely high pay (although as we have seen from the respective salaries of MBA graduates from different institutions, it carries healthy financial benefits on the way up the ladder).

They may argue instead that high educational achievement is merely a frequent and important aid to individual progression into the jobs where extremely high pay is awarded. They might say that it is consistent high performance, possibly in conjunction with high educational achievement, which makes an individual "talented".

A high level of proven performance is the second common interpretation of "talent". So will such performance be "tomorrow's source of competitive advantage"? One's instinctive response might be: of course it is! But remember, we are not talking about collective or organisational performance here; we are talking about individual performance. Is individual performance, of a sufficiently high standard to justify the term "talented" and the financial rewards this definition sometimes entails, the primary source of competitive advantage for a company?

The first problem here is identifying the high level of individual performance. If we can't identify it, we can't reward it or strive to retain it, and the talent ideology becomes meaningless. If a small group of individuals are behind your company's success, but you don't know who they are, how do you know they are behind your company's success?

Once again, we have to come back to the problem of measurability. The talent ideology, in my view embraced opportunistically to exploit a lack of measurability in the knowledge economy, is, on closer examination, undermined by exactly the same thing. As Peter Drucker once remarked: "If you can't measure it, you can't manage it." Quite so.

Second, many would agree with Gladwell that a company's success relies more heavily on factors unrelated to the performance of a few individuals, such as efficient systems or a high level of workforce commitment, or even external factors, such as the state of the economy or a serendipitous demand for the company's products. In the words of Charles de Gaulle, "the graveyards are full of indispensable men." The world still manages to revolve on its axis.

There is a third point to raise here. We also have to address the issue of rarity and potential replaceability. Even if we can make a clear case that a small minority of individuals are responsible for making a considerable positive impact on company performance, the argument for high pay has still not been won.

Let's take an individual in the corporate world who does work in a transparent and measurable role. Perhaps a salesperson who works in a very small team or on his own, and consistently sells more over a substantial period of time than his colleagues or his counterparts in competitor firms that have similar market clout. It might appear that there is a good case for high pay. If high revenue and profits are sloshing round the industry in which the salesperson operates, then it might appear that there is a good case for extremely high pay.

Even in this very rare case of substantial and proven measurable value, we must raise the question of how easy or difficult it would be to replace that person. Unlike in the case of the soccer star Messi, there are two pools of people, one very sizeable, one even more so, from which an adequate replacement for the salesperson could potentially be found.

The very sizeable pool consists of excellent and proven salespeople in other industries, perhaps where the available revenue and profits are lower. To make a leap between industries, all that salesperson needs to acquire is product or market knowledge. Many people within any industry, not just the allegedly talented, will possess such knowledge. Acquiring them does not therefore require rare skill. The rare skill is the art of selling, not the ability to digest specialist information, and is therefore not industry-specific.

Messi's counterparts in other sports, on the other hand, could not potentially replace him. Kobe Bryant, the great Los Angeles Lakers basketball player, could not emulate Messi's feats, and the same could be said vice versa. The rare ability here is not the ability to play any sport well, but the particular sport in question.

The second, larger pool consists of motivated and otherwise impressive individuals who have never tried to sell anything. How do we know that there aren't many potentially excellent salespeople out there, maybe even in the same company as the proven sales "talent"? How much would it cost to test some, identify the best, provide them with some experience and teach them the relevant product and market knowledge? Any temptation to reward salespeople with eye-watering sums should be mitigated by asking these two questions.

Superiority Complex

The second pillar of the talent ideology contends that an increasingly complex global economy would require leaders with the rare ability to manage a company within that complex environment. This would appear to be a major justification for the doubling of the share of profits channelled into senior executive compensation in US public companies since 1980. Managing companies has become more difficult, the argument goes, and therefore fewer people can do it well.

Certainly, one can hear the words "complex" and "complexity" a great deal in descriptions of large companies, encouraging us to switch off our brains, bow to the orthodoxy and accept that only a tiny few could possibly live with so many diverse and intellectually demanding business areas and challenges.

Pay consultants Ira Kay and Steven van Putten provide an example of this approach: "In a fully comprehensive labor market", they write, "top CEO talent aspires to run larger, more complex companies. As company size and complexity increase, so, too, does CEO pay."

But what has changed in the nature of the economy since 1980 to justify such pay increases to those "comfortable with complexity"?

There has undoubtedly been a trend towards globalisation and product diversification among large companies, and technological change has been rapid. No CEO is expected to be an expert in all countries in which the company does business, in all products the company sells, and in all relevant technology the company exploits. But he should ideally be able to construct a coherent overview of the key elements of each, and how they all interrelate.

This is without doubt a considerable intellectual challenge. But even if it were true that only a tiny few could overcome this challenge, and the vast majority of all those very intelligent people with high IQs and excellent commercial experience couldn't quite grasp that level of complexity, how on earth then do you find that tiny few? How do you measure the supposedly extraordinarily rare ability to prevail against extreme complexity?

I would venture that companies really don't know the answer to that question either, and that most don't even try to establish what would inevitably be a very fallible test to measure individual comfort with complexity. Instead they appoint one of many seemingly equally qualified individuals from below the top tier inside the company, who might appear to have successfully dealt with some complexity, but not as much complexity as the CEO will face.

Whom do they choose of these seemingly equally qualified candidates? Who else but the one who has made the most powerful alliances within the company, who most looks the part and who will fit the most seamlessly into the exclusive club? Of all the directors in Fortune 500 companies in 2008, only 15 per cent were women, and just over 3 per cent were "women of colour". Just 24, or 2.4 per cent, of the Fortune 1000 CEOs in 2008 were women.

In his book "Blink", Malcolm Gladwell examined the height of CEOs of large companies. In the general American population, about 14.5 per cent of all men are six feet or over. Among CEOs of the Fortune 500 companies he looked at, that proportion is 58 per cent. Even more strikingly, around 1 in 30 adult American men are 6'2" or taller, but among CEOs, that proportion is around 1 in 3.

Can we take corporate mouthing of the talent ideology seriously when so many of those deemed sufficiently talented to get their heads round complexity are tall, white men between 45 and 65?

Another approach may be to hire a CEO from another company who appears to have successfully dealt with complexity – that is, if you don't take the view that he merely benefited from, say, a booming economy, or for whatever reason unrelated to any ability to deal with complexity.

In other words, if companies genuinely believe that the ability to attain mastery over the complexity of the modern corporation and its challenges is extremely rare, then their quest to find the qualified individual will be little more, once again, than a stab in the dark.

Extinct Executives

The final pillar of the talent ideology relates to demography. As the Western population become older, the number of people in the prime of their working life is declining, and with it the supply of potentially talented workers and executives. This alleged reduction in potential executive talent is another available justification for higher pay.

"The number of 35-to-44 year-olds in the United States will decline by 15 percent between 2000 and 2015," proclaims the "War for Talent" article. "Moreover", it continues, "no countervailing trends are apparent. Women are no longer surging into the workforce, white-collar productivity improvements have flattened, immigration levels are stable, and executives are not prolonging their careers."

The demography argument might hold good if large international companies were intending to recruit all their executive "talent" from the traditional sources of North America and Western Europe. In these regions, the populations are undoubtedly ageing and will need to be reinforced by large-scale immigration to strengthen the economy, and in Europe's case, to help pay to maintain public health and pension systems.

But the fact is that several regions of the world have undergone, or are currently undergoing, a gradual Westernisation of their economy and working practices. Eastern Europe, India, China, the rest of Asia and Latin America are all now potential sources of able and suitable recruits. An estimated 1.2 million engineers and scientists graduate every year in China and India alone, as many as in the United States, the European Union and Japan combined.

There are abundant local opportunities in all these regions to gain work experience in international companies, master the international language of business (English) and study for the Western-style business degrees which companies often value.

These candidates from emerging markets will thus be increasingly immersed in Western business mores, yet perhaps in a better position to understand the cultural intricacies of a global business than a North American who has never lived elsewhere, or who has spent an obligatory three-year stint in a hermetic ex-pat community somewhere abroad. Perhaps they can aspire more realistically to the "multicultural fluency" referred to by the McKinsey authors.

According to projections, some of these regions will also experience rapidly falling birthrates and their populations will consequently age. That is not the relevant point here. The fact is that the supply of potential "talent" available to large, international companies is increasing, not decreasing, because these regions were not Westernised previously and are now becoming so. Increased supply should, in theory, therefore act to reduce the cost of high-ranking employees – that is, their pay.

Some may counter that despite some Westernisation, candidates from these countries have not yet sufficiently adapted to established business methods. McKinsey conducted a survey of human resources professionals on this issue, asking them to rate the employability of graduates from various emerging markets.

Respondents reckoned that they could only possibly hire 3 per cent of Chinese graduates, 8 per cent of Brazilians and 10 per cent of Russians for a generalist position, even if there was sufficient demand to hire every candidate. "Poor English skills, dubious educational qualifications, and cultural issues—such as a lack of experience on teams and a reluctance to take initiative or assume leadership roles—were among the problems most frequently cited," declared the report.

Is this the instinctive response of vulnerable incumbent knowledge workers seeking to protect their position? How many graduates anywhere have extensive experience of teams or an urge to assume leadership roles? Cynicism aside, it is anyhow likely that a similar survey conducted in another twenty, perhaps ten, maybe even five years will produce vastly different results.

In a Wilson Quarterly article analyzing the latest United Nations demographic projections, the author, Martin Walker, concluded:

"China's new middle class, defined as those in households with incomes above about $10,000 a year, is now estimated to number between 100 million and 150 million people. Some put the figure in India as high as 200 million. But it is apparent from the urban landscape across the developing world whether in Mumbai or Shanghai, São Paulo or Moscow, Dubai or Istanbul – that a growing proportion of consumers seek to emulate a Western-international lifestyle, which includes an air-conditioned house with a car in the garage, a private garden, satellite TV, and Internet access, along with the chance to raise a limited number of children, all of whom will have the opportunity to go to college."

Somehow, it doesn't seem likely that sufficiently able executives will soon go the way of the dodo.

Actions Speak Louder

The original definition of talent may be unclear, and the theory itself may be far from convincing, but this is all somewhat irrelevant anyway. The available evidence appears to confirm that the talent ideology's appeal has less to do with its highly questionable content, and more to do with the self-interest of high-flyers. Polls of senior executives suggest that although they pay a great deal of lip service to "talent", especially during the recent boom period, they don't spend much time thinking about it or establishing practical strategies relating to it.

Take this poll as a typical example. In a joint 2008 survey by the consultancy Development Dimensions International and the Economist Intelligence Unit, 55 per cent of respondents, all senior executives in global companies, said that their firms' performance was "likely" or "very likely" to suffer in the near future due to "insufficient leadership talent".

Despite this opinion, only one in five said they often spent time on "managing leadership talent", and only one in ten often "review leadership talent with the board". An identical proportion to those who viewed "insufficient leadership talent" as a major short-term problem – 55 per cent – rarely or never "review leadership talent with the board".

Even ignoring any possible element of self-deception in such surveys, with people giving the answers they feel they ought to, the reality anyway is that executive attention to "talent" is manifestly limited. Yes, yes, it's all-important, we really care about talent, we're losing sleep over it, if we don't act now we could go down the pan, but do we actually lift a finger to do anything about it? You got me there!

Some might say that senior executives have short-term horizons that are incompatible with a focus on talent. Their pay is usually based on short-term results, and the availability of sufficient talent is perhaps more of a long-term strategic issue for companies. Therefore, the argument might go: executives do genuinely believe in the tenets of the talent ideology, but they have little personal incentive to do anything about it.

However, the results of this survey contradict this argument. More than one half of respondents believe that their company will suffer in the "near future" due to "insufficient leadership talent". Their own short-term individual reward would therefore be likely to decrease as a result of this poorer company performance, yet they still don't act. One can conclude that they don't really believe in the importance of "talent" at all, and that they are constantly talking about it for other reasons.

Re-enter McKinsey. In a 2008 article written to mark the tenth anniversary of the original landmark piece, the company reported the results of its own, more recent, global surveys on executive attitudes to "talent".

"The first, in 2006, revealed that the respondents regarded finding talented people as the single most important managerial preoccupation for the rest of this decade," wrote the McKinsey authors. "The second, conducted in 2007, revealed that nearly half of all respondents expect intensifying competition for talent – and the increasingly global nature of that competition – to have a major effect on their companies over the next five years. No other global trend was considered nearly as significant."

However, a little later in the same article, we learn that 59 per cent of executives in a further McKinsey survey reckon that senior managers not spending "enough high-quality time on talent management" is the greatest obstacle to good talent management. No other global trend was considered nearly as significant; the single most important managerial preoccupation for the rest of this decade. For such a major preoccupation, there does seem to be precious little preoccupying going on.

Why is there such a gap between what senior executives say and what they do? A few, related, reasons come to mind. To reiterate a point already made, the emphasis on the concept, rather than the action, has much to do with associating the relevant individual or leadership team with the word "talent" and little to do with a genuine belief.

Constantly harping on about "talent" signals a progressive mindset, but the necessary urge to implement a meaningful talent strategy is largely absent because, when it all comes down to it, these senior executives don't really believe in the concept in any practicable way.

The second reason is that purposeful action on "talent" would threaten the currently successful but permanently vulnerable. If a talent strategy were to have any substance at all, it would surely introduce or strengthen a culture of meritocracy. The practical reality of meritocracy, a system in which advancement is based on individual ability or achievement, would appear more attractive to those at the bottom than to those at the top.

Those at the bottom with talent have the most to gain from it, while those at the top without talent have most to lose. Meanwhile, those at the top who do have talent have little to gain from meritocracy (they are already at the top). When you add all this together, it follows that corporate hierarchies, where so much power rests at the top, naturally militate against the emergence of genuine meritocracy.

Investing the time and effort to create a workable and comprehensible definition of talent might just conceivably end up with the company leadership being judged as not up to the mark. If you're already at the top, investing the time and effort may not therefore seem so appealing. The reason why executives pay such little practical attention to "talent" is not because it doesn't chime with their short-term personal interests. That is barking up the wrong tree. They pay such little practical attention to "talent" because it is a potential threat to both their short-term and long-term interests.

Following from this point, the "all talk, no action" approach is also perfectly designed to boost pay. It creates the strong impression that there is a desperate need for people of a certain high calibre, similar to the current incumbents, but lacks the real substance to create the competition that might threaten the high income of those incumbents. The intended result is higher pay for the incumbents, without really having to fight to retain it.

One could argue, of course, that it is within the interests of senior executives to surround themselves with the best available people. After all, they might improve the overall performance of the company, possibly improving senior executive pay as a result. They will also be capable of planning and executing important projects, thus helping to relieve the burden of work on those above them in the hierarchy.

Indeed, those senior executives who are most confident in their own ability very probably do attempt to promote the absolute best (if they think they can work out who they are). But many others will instinctively shy away from this course of action, knowing deep down that very good people might soon compare favourably to those who appointed them, thereby presenting a threat to their incumbency.

The third explanation for executive inaction is that people cannot act on something they don't understand, and have no particular desire to understand. To be fair, there may well be a genuine but vague notion among some executives that "talent" is important. But press them on what they actually mean, and they are likely to reply with a hodgepodge of meaningless language, or scuttle off to concentrate on something they do understand, like profits, balance sheets, their own pay or their own career.

Untalented Ingredients

Unmasking the talent ideology is only one part of the battle against high pay; the next part is to understand how company performance relies on factors, usually downplayed, that have little to do with the efforts of a small circle of allegedly talented individuals.

CHAPTER 3

Neglected Terrain

In July 2001, Stan O'Neal was appointed as president and chief operating officer of Merrill Lynch, after impressive stints in various senior roles at the company. Less than 18 months later, he became the chief executive, the first African-American to head a major Wall Street brokerage firm. The grandson of a former slave, spending his youth picking cotton and corn on the family farm in Alabama during segregation, O'Neal's ascent appeared to symbolise the triumph of individual talent in a modern, meritocratic society.

Ensconced in his executive positions, the Harvard MBA graduate set about pursuing a company-wide cost-cutting programme with what was described in the Financial Times as "ruthless efficiency". The company laid off 24,000 employees (fully one third of the workforce), including several prominent senior executives, shut down operations in several countries, closed hundreds of offices, and reduced extravagant perks such as gourmet food for top managers. O'Neal admitted at the time that his public image was "some sort of Quasimodo, prowling around the dungeons of Merrill Lynch, torturing costs out of the system."

The hard-nosed strategy appeared to pay off. Performing relatively poorly at the turn of the millennium, Merrill's financial results later soared with O'Neal at the helm. Profits for 2003 reached nearly $4 billion, a record for the company, only to be bettered each year until they surpassed $7 billion in 2006. The company's stock price at one time doubled in the space of twelve months.

The business media cooed. Rejecting one analyst's description of O'Neal as a "classic bean counter", Fortune magazine journalist David Rynecki argued that "there is another description for Merrill's CEO – and this one is, frankly, more accurate: turnaround genius. Fact is, this hard-charging, steel-plated leader may have saved one of the great Wall Street institutions from extinction."

James Gorman, a former senior consultant at McKinsey and then president of Merrill's Global Private Client group, joined in the chorus of praise: "Stan was made CEO at the ultimate moment of truth," he said. "Our world was imploding, and he had the courage to make difficult decisions. If that's not heroic, I don't what is."

Merrill's financial success led to huge, and increasing, financial rewards for O'Neal. From 2003 to 2006, his total annual compensation was (in chronological order): $28 million, $32 million, $37 million and $46 million. Or $145 million over four years, or about $100,000 a day.

In 2007, however, his professional reputation suffered a decline of quite dramatic proportions. During his tenure as chief executive, Merrill had significantly expanded its activity in various business areas, such as foreign exchange dealing and commodity trading. The mortgage department also grew, with the company hiring a team from Credit Suisse that specialised in collateralised debt obligations – asset-backed securities that may be supported by any type of debt, including mortgage bonds. Merrill also bought a mortgage company, First Franklin, which had issued home loans worth more than $29 billion in 2005.

It was this exposure to the mortgage market, and specifically to the more risky subprime sector of this market, that served to wreck

O'Neal's public standing. In the third quarter of 2007, Merrill declared a write-down of almost $8 billion related to mortgage securities.

A week after this announcement, O'Neal had resigned, although the personal blow was somewhat cushioned by a payout estimated at $162 million in company stock and retirement benefits. One year later, Bank of America stepped in to buy the ailing company, allegedly because it had been placed under severe pressure from a US government that was deeply concerned about the potential effect of Merrill going the same way as the bankrupt Lehman Brothers.

O'Neal was ridiculed for playing twenty rounds of golf in six weeks while Merrill was facing catastrophe. "As Merrill's losses mounted", wrote the journalist Michael Lewis, "we know exactly where Chief Executive Officer Stan O'Neal was, what he was doing, and with whom: On a golf course. Golfing. By himself."

Jim Cramer, the host of CNBC's "Mad Money" television programme, argued that O'Neal should not have been allowed to resign, writing that "this was the most compelling case for a firing that I've ever come across that didn't involve outright embezzlement." In 2009, Portfolio Magazine assembled a panel of professors from top business schools and asked them to name their worst American CEOs of all time. O'Neal was number 18 on their list.

This was really some comedown. In a matter of one year, O'Neal had descended from heroic genius, a Churchill-figure, to a laughing-stock dunce, one of the worst chief executives in corporate history. How can this drastic turnaround in perception be explained?

Talent and the Halo Effect

In his book, "*The Halo Effect*", Phil Rosenzweig argues that analysis of the reasons for company performance is often flawed, being based on little more than the natural human tendency to derive specific conclusions from a general impression.

"When a company is doing well, with rising profits and a soaring share price, most people infer that it has a brilliant strategy, a visionary leader, a motivated workforce, strong execution skills, and more," he writes. "But when that same company falters, observers are quick to make the opposite attributions: they say that the strategy was misguided, the leader became arrogant, the people were complacent, execution was sloppy, and more. In fact, little may have changed."

What Rosenzweig doesn't discuss is the extent to which top executives in the corporate world stand to gain from this "halo effect", and the extent, therefore, to which this powerful group has helped to preserve and protect its influence. The group's allies – pay consultants, management consultants, institutional shareholders, business schools, headhunters, sycophantic and ambitious subordinates, the business writers whose readers comprise all the aforementioned, and others – have all been keen to assist in this process through peddling the talent ideology.

This ideology, devised and trumpeted by high-flying employees for the benefit of high-flying employees, has augmented the halo effect, or more specifically, the notion that the leader or leadership team is the all-important factor determining corporate performance. It is not only laziness or simple-mindedness that leads us to attribute the success of an organisation to the rare abilities of its leadership. The pervasiveness of the talent ideology demands that we do.

Some may counter that leaders can both win and lose from the "halo effect", and therefore its existence is not necessarily in their interests. As Rosenzweig points out, there is an equal tendency to blame the leader when things go wrong, as there is to heap praise on him when things go well.

But as was the case with O'Neal, the talent ideology invariably works in favour of executives, in terms of pay, whether they succeed and get lionised, or fail and get pilloried. After all, they are in an ideal position to negotiate a contract that will protect them in the event of their company failing.

One might wonder why, if they are so talented, they should feel the need to be protected in this way. But the talented leader, believed to possess such uncommon and valuable attributes, is not so easy to bargain down. So O'Neal earned $145 million in four years when the company's performance was good, a vast figure only to be bettered by his payout when it nosedived.

The differing popularity of the various attributions made for corporate success reveals the considerable impact that the talent ideology and its supporters have made on the "halo effect".

There are certainly business books that explain company success in terms of its "motivated workforce" or "strong execution skills", as Rosenzweig puts it, often written by consultants-cum-writers who then benefit by selling their ideas to the corporate world on how this can be achieved. But there are a good many more books and articles that highlight the role of the "visionary leader" or the "brilliant strategy", itself no doubt the brainchild of the "visionary leader".

It may be, as Rosenzweig says, that "the halo effect is a very common mental shortcut that is born out of a natural desire for simplicity". But there are other explanations for corporate success that appear to me to be equally simple as the leadership or talent explanation – a buoyant economy, an industry where only a few players dominate a market with rising demand, a product that happens to be very popular – which somehow don't get the same attention.

The Economy, Stupid

When bankers in Wall Street and the City of London made large amounts of money, we were told that this was a consequence of their talent. In fact, despite the 2008 global financial crisis and the severe recession that followed, we are still told the same thing about those areas of the banking industry that continue to make large amounts of money, or have since recovered their performance.

In mid-2009, the pay consultants, Johnson Associates, predicted that bonuses may rise by up to 30 per cent from the previous year in equities and fixed-income businesses on Wall Street. This prediction came just a matter of months after the financial chaos of the previous autumn.

In September 2008, Goldman Sachs received a $10 billion rescue loan from the US government. A few months later, it set aside more than $11 billion for employee pay for the first half of 2009, and was on course for an average annual payout per worker in excess of $600,000. This figure would virtually equal their payout per worker for 2007, a record year.

The usual suspects queued up to issue their justifying mantras. "Wall Street is being realistic," said Sandy Gross, managing partner of Pinetum Partners, an executive search firm specialising in the finance sector. "You have to retain your human capital."

But what if Ms Gross, and the many people who agree with her, have missed the point here? What if it is the economic environment that is far and away the predominant cause of the revenue that banks generate, and the company's people in fact matter very little?

What if it isn't talented employees that create investment banking revenue, but inevitable investment banking revenue that creates the mirage of talented employees? Perhaps the "halo effect" is firmly rooted within the entire culture of investment banking, and within external perceptions of the industry, and people often wrongly attribute huge revenue to the existence of a talented workforce, an impression that is then energetically reinforced by those who stand to gain from it.

Perhaps, indeed, it is not MBAs from top business schools that create banking revenue, but banking revenue which promotes the perception that MBAs from top business schools are commercially valuable. This perception then raises their pay, thus ensuring that few companies outside banks can afford them. Banks are thereby rendered more or less free to recruit the pick of these MBAs, in this way benefiting from an association with the brands of top business schools which their own inevitable revenue has significantly boosted.

The same mirage also serves to raise barriers to entry to the industry, protecting the position of the highly-paid but vulnerable incumbents. Because it is believed that only graduates from a small group of top universities and business schools can create such revenue (hence their high pay), graduates from other institutions are denied the opportunity to threaten their incumbency.

Let's look at global investment banking revenue since 1997. Starting off at $37 billion, industry revenue grew to $57 billion by 2000 with the dotcom boom, then fell back down to $34 billion in 2002 with the dotcom bust. It then grew substantially throughout the subsequent boom years, to a peak of $84 billion in 2007. Then, with the industry's losses in the subprime market and the global economic slowdown, revenue fell by 30 per cent in 2008, to $59 billion.

Throughout this period, as revenue rose and fell with the vagaries of the economy, pay within the sector more or less did the same, with around 50 per cent of revenue at investment banks persistently allocated to employees. (Incidentally, this figure is quite similar to the percentage paid to players in the "Big Four" American team sports and to soccer players at some major English league clubs, where recipients, as we shall see later, do undoubtedly possess a rare talent.)

During the bad times, this proportion might even go up, with especially poorly performing banks seeking to retain those they perceive to be their key employees. For example, Morgan Stanley was expected to pay their workforce 68 per cent of revenue during 2009 to ward off poaching from competitors.

Bankers' pay, and the extent to which they are viewed as "talented", tends to go up and down with the economy. When one sees this pattern clearly, the Stan O'Neal story starts to look a little different. Merrill performed well in the boom years from 2003, and then performed very badly along with most of the rest of the industry as the 2008 financial crisis took hold. O'Neal's fortunes followed his company's, which in turn followed the economy's (although, maybe, not quite – if you count his $162 million payoff).

We were told that O'Neal was a man amongst men, and the next minute we were told he was a callous buffoon. Confused? Let's try a more consistent narrative instead.

O'Neal was largely a beneficiary and victim of circumstance, a passive player, a leaf in the wind buffeted by the elements. Yes, he launched a cost-cutting strategy that appeared successful in the short term. But a great number of chief executives have followed a similar course, and would have followed it in his situation. The course was, after all, a natural and logical response to excessive expenses.

Yes, the company he led invested in a sector that was to prove disastrous. But, to a greater or lesser extent, so did the entire investment banking industry.

Whether he had talent or not was irrelevant. He just happened to be the incumbent, the head of a company that was performing, more or less, as it would have done with a different leader, selected from a large pool of equally qualified candidates from both within Merrill Lynch and outside the company. He was not a hero, and he was not a dunce. He was just there.

Ignoring the Inconvenient

Let's now turn to industry structure and how this might affect company performance. Take the example of an oligopoly, a market form in which an industry is dominated by a very small number of competitors. It provides another plausible explanation for a company's success that has nothing to do with individual talent.

In May 2009, nearly 60 per cent of shareholders at the oil company Royal Dutch Shell voted against the company's pay plan for its top executives. It marked the largest shareholder revolt in UK corporate history, larger indeed than the 38 per cent of shareholders of its rival, BP, who had voted against their own company's pay plan one month earlier.

What had irked both sets of shareholders was the companies' insistence on rewarding top executives despite the failure to reach preordained targets. Shell and BP are two of the six largest, non-state energy companies in the world, collectively known as the "supermajors". The preordained targets related to comparative performance vis-à-vis rival "supermajors". If these targets had been reached, then top executives were due to receive additional rewards.

In BP's case, directors were awarded a discretionary bonus for 2008, despite the company being at the bottom of its peer group in terms of total shareholder return. Tony Hayward, the chief executive who had risen through the ranks since joining the company as a graduate in 1982, received bonus shares worth £336,000 ($570,000), in addition to the £2.5 million ($4.25 million) he received in salary and cash bonus.

Shell's remuneration policy measured total shareholder returns, for the period 2006 to 2008, against those attained by four of its rivals – BP, ExxonMobil, Chevron and Total. Ranking first would have meant that directors qualified for shares worth 200 per cent of their salary, down to 80 per cent if the company ranked in third position, but nothing for below third.

In the end, the company ranked fourth. According to the agreed formula, therefore, Shell's top five executives did not qualify for any payout at all. However, the remuneration committee decided to award these executives half of what they would have received if the company had been ranked in third position.

Jeroen van der Veer, the chief executive who had joined the company straight after military service (in the Netherlands) in 1971, received shares worth £1.25 million ($2.1 million). His total package for 2008 amounted to £9.2 million ($15.6 million).

BP defended its decision to ignore the terms of its own pay plan by citing the company's "excellent operational performance." Meanwhile, a Shell spokesman justified the payment on similar grounds, emphasising that the company's underlying operating performance had been strong during

2008, and pointing out it had only been narrowly beaten into third place by Total in the relevant rankings. Although the company's representatives were keen to declare publicly that they would "take the outcome of this (shareholders') vote very seriously", they also stressed that the vote was merely "advisory" and would not disqualify the pay award.

Imperfect Competition

What can we say about these two stories? First, we note the rather casual detachment of the companies' remuneration committees, which were determined to award bonuses to executives even though their shareholders had either been significantly opposed to it, or had actually voted against it.

To summarise the facts, Mr. Hayward and Mr. van der Veer were both awarded several million dollars in just one year because their companies attained what was portrayed as success in absolute terms, and despite those companies failing to achieve what had been defined by their own remuneration committees as success in relative terms.

But one could argue that the structure of the oil industry meant that both the absolute success and even the relative success (which was not attained) were not particularly onerous targets for the companies to achieve. And that is before we even enter into the question about whether the chief executive or his colleagues had much influence on the eventual outcome anyway.

Let's look at the absolute performance first – the "strong" or "excellent" operating results that company representatives have told us about. It is true that BP and Shell both declared record profits for 2008, with BP up by 39 per cent to $25.6 billion and Shell up by 14 per cent to $31.4 billion (close to $100 million a day).

But here again, as with the investment banks, oil companies had largely capitalised on external economic factors that were almost entirely beyond their control. Profits in the oil industry tend to rise and fall with the price of crude oil and the level of consumer demand. When the price of oil goes up, companies can still extract crude at a relatively constant cost, but sell it at higher prices. With the increasing price of oil (it had risen dramatically in the period up to and including 2008), the profits of BP and Shell had soared. Like O'Neal, Hayward and van der Veer were the principal individual beneficiaries of an extremely helpful environment.

Indeed, with the onset of recession, decreasing demand and lower oil prices, Shell's profits for the first quarter of 2009 fell by 58 per cent compared to the same period the previous year, and BP's were 62 per cent lower.

What about the relative performance? Would Shell directors have deserved an additional bonus equivalent to four fifths of their salary if the company had been ranked third in the relevant rankings? Third place out of five is the median position, and one would not rationally assume that an average company performance should be a trigger for a multi-million dollar personal payment.

Even if Shell had been ranked first, which would have entailed a payout equivalent to twice the executives' salary and therefore added even more substantially to the recipients' already burgeoning personal wealth, any urge to eulogise the leadership ought to have been tempered by the reality that there were only four rivals.

It would surely be difficult to classify this business environment as highly competitive, of the type experienced by so many entrepreneurs and small businesses in their everyday dealings. As well as the very small number of direct competitors, the barriers to entry to the industry are practically insurmountable. A person in the street could not hope to set up a business that could ultimately challenge the "supermajors". To extract oil, you need vast financial strength (the five companies in the rankings had a combined market value of \$854 billion in 2009), technological expertise throughout the organisation and permits from governments.

So we can argue, therefore, that Mr. van der Veer received close to $15 million in just one year, in addition to the many millions he had already received in previous years, because the company which happened to employ him operated in an environment that guaranteed huge revenue, and despite the fact that it failed to reach the minimum target of a series in which even the achievement of the maximum target would be hard to classify as exceptional.

To put matters into further perspective, Mr. van der Veer was but one of 102,000 Shell employees, operating in an industry where investment in oil exploration can take many years to pay off.

How are we to measure his relative contribution vis-à-vis such a large number of colleagues, past and present? As Spencer Clark, a high-ranking General Electric executive during the much-exalted reign of Jack Welch, said of his former boss: "Jack did a good job, but everyone seems to forget that the company had been around for over a hundred years before he ever took the job, and he had 70,000 other people to help him."

Did van der Veer's own personal strategies lead to the company's inevitably high absolute performance and below-average comparative performance? Or was it predominantly the strategies of his predecessors prior to his appointment as chief executive in October 2004 that led to these results?

Several other industries are also heavily dominated by a very small number of companies. Examples of these oligopolies include:

Global Aircraft Manufacturers: Boeing (CEO James McNerney 2008 total compensation – $14.8 million) and Airbus (part of EADS)

Newswire Services: Thomson Reuters (CEO Tom Glocer 2008 total compensation – $ 36.6 million) and Bloomberg (private company – pay details unavailable)

Global Insurance Brokers: Marsh (CEO Daniel Glaser 2008 total compensation – $9.8 million) and Aon (CEO Greg Case 2008 total compensation – $12.9 million)

Happenstance

When asked what worried him the most, the then British Prime Minister, Harold Macmillan, replied: "Events, dear boy, events." He was not the first political leader to let his guard down and admit the huge role of serendipity in the perception of their success. Some 150 years before, Napoleon Bonaparte had supposedly said that he sought neither brilliant nor courageous generals, but "lucky" ones.

Honest corporate leaders would surely say something similar. External events, or discoveries, can lead to dramatic rises or falls in sales of a particular product, or a group of products, that can have a substantial effect on corporate performance.

For example, scientific research over recent years has pointed to the myriad health benefits of omega-3 fats, such as a reduced risk of heart disease and certain cancers, or improved brain performance. The consumption of oily fish, other omega-3-enriched food and omega-3 supplements has increased dramatically as a result. Sales of food and beverages that contain the nutrient amounted to $100 million in the United States in 2002, but are projected to climb 70-fold to $7 billion by 2011.

In this example, many different companies, selling food or health supplements, will have benefited from these discoveries about omega-3. The pharmaceutical industry, on the other hand, functions with a different model.

The patent system, established to strengthen the incentive for innovation, allows one company to market a new product without competition for a certain time. This system renders each individual company more susceptible to volatile fluctuations in profitability caused by health scares relating to a particular drug, or by reports confirming its health benefits. As such, the industry presents a number of clear examples showing how sudden unforeseen shifts in external demand for a particular product can boost or undermine corporate performance.

Avandia is the brand name for an anti-diabetic drug launched in 1999 by the pharmaceutical company, GlaxoSmithKline. The drug allows the body to use its own insulin more effectively, thereby helping to reduce blood sugar levels. The patent for the drug is due to expire in 2012.

Sales of the drug were outstanding during its first few years, peaking at £1.4 billion ($2.4 billion) in 2006. It became GSK's second-best seller, with around 6 per cent of the company's total turnover and with sales still growing strongly.

But in 2007, a report published in the New England Journal of Medicine collated various data to conclude that Avandia significantly increased the likelihood of heart attacks and death by cardiovascular diseases. Sales of the drug fell by almost two thirds in the period after the release of the report, to £512 million ($870 million) in 2008.

The year 2007 could have been a good one for the company, with several other products showing rapid sales growth. But this progress was offset by the failure of Avandia, and company turnover increased by just 2 per cent, compared with 9 per cent the previous year. The perception of GSK's potential for future earnings growth was also adversely affected. By the company's own admission, the fortunes of its stock price reflected concerns about Avandia, falling by 5 per cent during 2007, compared to an overall increase in the FTSE 100 index of 4 per cent.

Who should we blame for Avandia's drop in fortunes and the resulting negative impact on the company's performance? Perhaps we should blame the company's chief executive at the time, Jean-Pierre Garnier, the Stanford MBA who retired with a promised annual pension of $1.3 million in 2008, a year in which his total compensation reached nearly $20 million? The same chief executive, one might add as an aside, whose company's stock price almost halved under his stewardship.

But it would be just as unfair to blame Mr. Garnier for the Avandia story, as it would be to blame him for the company's performance during his tenure as CEO, when the pharmaceutical industry as a whole was struggling with increasing drug development costs, declining drug discovery rates and the patent expiry of best-selling products.

After all, Avandia was launched in 1999 prior to him taking the leadership reins. Even if he had been in charge at the time, his role would surely not have encompassed marshalling the detail of the pre-market clinical trials that would have been necessary to satisfy the regulators.

Nor would it be entirely fair to blame the doubtless well-paid senior managers of the company's huge research and development department, whose own initial investigations did not uncover the extent of the problems with the drug. It took the much more extensive sample comprising millions of eventual users to reveal the alleged risks of Avandia.

Indeed, the presence or absence of individual talent appears to have little to do with the outcome of this story. More probably, the story serves as a very typical instance of a change in company fortunes brought about by unpredictable circumstance – by events, dear boy, events.

Impregnable Brand

Neville Isdell was chief executive of The Coca-Cola Company from 2004 to 2008. His total compensation in his full years as CEO was $26.1 million in 2005, $20.9 million in 2006 and $21.6 million in 2007. Some reward for the Harvard graduate who had joined the company in Zambia in 1966, and then spent the best part of the subsequent four decades as an employee, steadily working his way up the ranks of the global Coke empire.

No doubt Mr. Isdell performed very competently as chief executive. He apparently ploughed more money into marketing, after listening to the concerns of his employees. Some may even go as far as to argue that other people in the same position might have ploughed more money into marketing if many employees were imploring them to do so.

Justifying his pay package for 2007, the company pointed to its business growth at a time when sales of traditional soft drinks were declining in the company's largest market (the United States), to Isdell's efforts in leading the company's efforts in corporate social responsibility, and to his work on succession planning.

"Everything else I've done is vitally important," preened the CEO when he later departed the company, "but having successful succession is the most important thing of all." Isdell believes that shareholders (you and I, just to remind you) paid him a large proportion of close to $100 million so that he could pass on the chief executive baton to someone else, whose principal role, presumably, will be to pass the same baton on to someone else. One could be forgiven for thinking that such logic is somewhat circular, and will doubtless continue ad infinitum, with individuals becoming supremely rich because they nominated someone else in their entourage to become supremely rich.

Let's try to attain some perspective on Isdell's acquisition of phenomenal personal wealth, which will have further augmented the considerable wealth he would already have accrued in other senior positions at the company. The Coca-Cola brand was first marketed in 1886, almost 60 years before Isdell was born in Northern Ireland. He became rich beyond the dreams of nearly every living person because he helped to administer, with the assistance of 92,400 colleagues, a brand that is so deeply rooted in our society that a 2009 study viewed it as the third most valuable in the world.

Indeed, in this study, Coca-Cola was ranked below only Google and Microsoft, two brand names that have only emerged in recent years and whose longevity over a number of decades has yet to be proven. We can say, therefore, that no brand is both as durable and as powerful as Coca-Cola.

One wonders what level of corporate performance would have been viewed as sufficiently poor to withhold the allocation of this phenomenal wealth to Isdell. A brand that durable and powerful was unlikely to sink without trace in the space of his four years at the helm. What reduction on the starting point of $21 billion of revenue in 2004 would have resulted in him receiving a lesser fortune, what reduction an even lesser fortune, and what reduction only a little fortune?

One could indeed argue that Isdell was sitting on a gold mine which he himself had played no part in discovering. One might also argue that his role in developing that gold mine is likely to have been extremely insignificant in the greater scheme of things, and is, in any case, completely immeasurable.

Where would Coca-Cola be now if Isdell, now in golfing retirement in Barbados on an estimated annual pension of $2.5 million, had declined for whatever reason to take up the role in 2004, and the vacant chief executive position assumed instead by any number of alternative and equally competent candidates? One might be tempted to suggest that you would still be seeing plenty of people drinking coca-cola in your local café.

Compare Mr. Isdell, and for that matter Mr. van der Veer, Mr. Hayward, Mr. O'Neal, Mr. Garnier, and all those other chief executives in large companies who have become so wealthy through administering well-established concerns, to the true entrepreneurs, the men and women who have forged a successful company from scratch, from nothing but a vague idea in their heads.

Going one step further, compare these CEOs to those who have not just forged a successful company from scratch, but an entire market from scratch. From Ray Kroc (McDonald's) to Pierre Omidyar (ebay), from Thomas Edison to Mark Zuckerberg (Facebook), these are the people who have deserved our admiration, and our money. With all their ingenuity, they spotted the potential gold mine, and with all their effort, they dug and developed it. Mr. Isdell may talk admiringly of his own achievements, but entrepreneurial success seems somewhat more "vitally important" to me.

A Matter of Engagement

So far in this chapter, I have written about some factors external to the company that influence the scale of corporate success – the state of the economy, market competition, chance events and an extremely durable consumer perception of the company's brand. But there are also factors within the company environment which might influence overall performance. Are these factors the consequence of individual talent, and more specifically, senior executive talent?

Important innovations, or an overall culture that encourages innovation, might explain corporate success. A disciplined focus on reducing costs, as implemented by Stan O'Neal, might also explain corporate success.

So might constant attention to efficient processes of production and service, as espoused by the eminent management writer and consultant, W. Edwards Deming, whose ideas are said to have made a great contribution to Japanese post-war economic success. "Costs go down and productivity goes up as improvement of quality is accomplished by better management of design, engineering, testing and by improvement of processes," wrote Deming.

There is no rare talent involved in cutting costs in an organisation. Many executives pursue that course quite successfully all the time. The Deming model is to be applied collectively, throughout an organisation. Individuals are secondary here; it is the system that counts.

What about innovation? A few people will have the capacity for ground-breaking ideas, but they are unlikely to stay for a long time within a large corporation. This is for three reasons.

First, ground-breaking ideas challenge the status quo. They are therefore likely to make the truly original thinker deeply unpopular with those who are doing well out of that status quo, thus hindering his or her progress up the ladder. "In every large-scale organization there is a natural tendency to discourage initiative and put a premium on conformity," suggested the management writer Peter Drucker, as far back as 1946. "Moreover, there is a danger in any large-scale organization for the older men at the top to be afraid and suspicious of talented or ambitious subordinates."

Second, the highly innovative individual might well react against the need to do things in a certain way when they, by definition, think those ways ought to be changed in some way. They might then leave the company out of frustration.

Third, he or she might well want to profit personally from their new ideas and set up their own business. They might then leave the company because they think they can do better outside it.

However, the broad term "innovation" might not only encompass ground-breaking ideas. It might also refer to the day-to-day creativity and imagination that many employees possess, helping their company to improve its products and processes on an ongoing basis. Many people might possess this potential, but fewer people might choose to use it. The choice, surely, depends on the individual employee's level of commitment to their job.

Some believe, therefore, that employee commitment, or to use the accepted jargon term, employee engagement, can explain the innovativeness and productivity of a company, and hence its overall performance.

Two questions need to be asked here in the context of this chapter. First, does employee engagement really affect company performance? And second, if it does, are senior executives responsible for creating the environment that fosters this valuable commodity, eliciting deserved financial reward in return?

Engagement will no doubt play a very considerable role in the respective success of two companies with, say, ten employees each, both selling identical products and with similar financial resources. Ten motivated employees are likely to produce better results than ten miserable ones, all other things being equal.

A brief glance at the history of sport would back this view.

Examples of teams of lower standing defeating teams packed full of proven individual talent in a one-off game occur quite regularly. There are also apparent instances of teams achieving success over a number of seasons with a group of individuals that seem no better, and perhaps even somewhat worse, than other groups in different teams that have achieved less success. Collective motivation has often been cited as the reason, although one does have to be a little wary of the halo effect here; Steve Archibald, a former Scottish soccer player, once said that team spirit is "an illusion glimpsed in victory."

Size and Commitment

What about the effect of employee motivation on large multinational companies? The first point to make is that they are surely too big to make company-wide generalisations about employee commitment across thousands of working teams and many different locations and countries, save in exceptional circumstances such as impending bankruptcy.

Take the examples used earlier. It is hard to believe that all Shell departments are more motivated than their BP counterparts, or vice versa. More likely, there are teams and individuals within all large companies that are highly motivated, and teams and individuals that are utterly uninterested, turn up, mess around and go home. Some companies have more of the former, and some more of the latter.

Indeed, Marcus Buckingham and his team of Gallup researchers discovered this phenomenon when they analysed the results of engagement surveys in more than 200 organisations. They found more variation within companies than between companies. In each of the organisations analysed, they saw some of the most engaged groups and some of the least engaged groups.

Top executives seemed none the wiser about this. "Few of the CEOs in our study could say which work units in their company were engaged effectively and which weren't," said Buckingham. "They didn't know where their culture was strong and where it was weak, whether it was getting better or getting worse — or how much this variation was costing."

Other studies have purported to prove that an organisation with a generally higher level of employee engagement performs better than an organisation with a lower one.

A 2006 Towers Perrin-ISR survey measured the engagement levels of 664,000 employees from more than fifty global multinational companies. One year later, it measured corporate financial performance, and found that companies with highly engaged employees outperformed those with less engaged staff by a very considerable margin over the twelve-month period. The former saw an average increase in net operating income of 19.2%, while the latter saw net operating income fall by an average of 32.7%.

Again, one has to take the halo effect into account. Rosenzweig looks at employee satisfaction ratings at Cisco – very high when the company was doing very well at the turn of the millennium, and much lower when performance plummeted and layoffs started. "Does employee satisfaction lead to high performance?" he asks. "Probably, but it's hard to say how much, and it turns out the reverse effect is stronger: Company performance is a more important determinant of employee satisfaction." And as we have seen, company performance often follows from such factors as the state of the economy, lack of competition, chance events and an impregnable brand name.

It could be that the companies which TowersPerrin-ISR revealed to be highly engaged were already performing well by the start of the twelve-month period, thus raising employee engagement, for example by paying people more, making their jobs more secure, or giving them more opportunities for training and personal career development.

However, we can't dismiss the findings completely. The sample is large and the discrepancy very significant. One might reasonably conclude: Some large companies have a higher proportion of highly-engaged employees and departments than others. The former companies are likely to perform better than the latter, all other things being equal. It may well also be that company performance, while being by some distance the principal determinant of overall employee engagement, is not the only one.

Cultural Phenomenon

If this is true, don't talented executives help in some small way to build employee morale, or corporate culture, and shouldn't they be handsomely rewarded for this contribution?

Management books, articles and case studies often imply, or state openly, that a chief executive is responsible for corporate culture. A large company's performance rises dramatically, a writer is sent to cover the story, and assorted employees flock to attribute the success to the transformation of the corporate culture planned and executed by the all-seeing, all-knowing CEO, a man blessed with the charisma to move mountains.

But an appreciation of the sheer size of these companies, together with Buckingham's conclusions (very different engagement levels within the same company), not to mention an acknowledgement of the "halo effect", makes this explanation appear extremely far-fetched.

Although he might well exert a positive or negative impact on the motivation of his senior management team, an American CEO sitting in Atlanta, Georgia, is very unlikely to have a direct influence on the attitude of a salesperson sitting thousands of miles away in Shanghai, whom he has never met. Much more convincing evidence indicates that it is the usually modestly-paid direct supervisor, and not the highly-paid distant senior executive, who represents the most powerful human influence on the day-to-day engagement of an employee.

For example, a 2005 article from The Journal of Applied Psychology, entitled "The Contagious Leader", reveals that the mood of the manager greatly affects the morale of his or her team. The best managers manage to lift themselves in order to lift others. Certainly, the influence of the team manager would help to explain Buckingham's findings.

Of course, the CEO and his supporters might well say that he is responsible for selecting the people beneath him, who are themselves responsible for selecting those beneath them, and so on. In other words, by the nature of the people he selects, he is responsible for setting the tone, the culture of the organisation. The argument goes that he would therefore influence, indirectly, the engagement of the Shanghai salesperson.

Suffice it to say there is no reliable evidence that this logic works in practice, so we are left to speculate. This is my speculation: A CEO might select his own team. Let's accept that he searches hard for certain clearly defined personality characteristics in the people directly beneath him, not just people he happens to like or know.

He might think that those eventually appointed possess the attributes he claims he wants, but his judgement in the selection process might have been flawed, and they might act differently once in their new position anyway. Likewise for the people selected in the tier below, and so on. If the CEO asserts that he influences, albeit indirectly, the attitude of the Shanghai salesperson at the very grassroots of the company, then this assertion demonstrates hubris and delusion of the highest order.

It is interesting to note, as a digression, that the talent ideology neglects the role of the inspiring people manager, preferring instead to concentrate on the virtues of the senior executive who is supposedly equipped to excel amid the complex demands of a sophisticated modern economy. Indeed, the middle management function has been largely decimated by the modern fashion of flat organisations, which have relatively few tiers of management.

But as we have already seen, the intention of the talent ideology is to further the interests of current high-fliers, not to improve company performance. And middle managers are, by definition, not high-fliers.

Away from Talent

In the previous two chapters, I have challenged the prevalent assumptions about individual talent, and its alleged impact on company performance. Before we move on to explore high pay in other fields, the next chapter digs deeper into the world of senior executives and finance workers, testing the other self-justifications used by the overpaid.

CHAPTER 4

The Gravy Train Engine

The arguments in defence of high corporate pay operate in three stages. First, we hear the argument that pay is an inevitable product of the market. This is an attempt to shut down the debate before it has started, by insinuating that people who dispute this statement are either childish naïfs, shameless populists or anti-business socialists.

If we probe a little deeper, the word "talent" is usually called upon as the next line of defence. As we have seen, what "talent" means is not adequately explained, and why it might be important (if we understood what it was) is not clear. But the intent, again, is to intimidate the curious-minded. "We, the insiders, value talented people, who happen, incidentally, to comprise our friends, people who pay us, and people who are like us. You, the outsiders, are not equipped with the experience and knowledge to know what we mean by talent."

That's where the defence of high pay normally stops. However, there are other arguments out there, articulated by those pushed a little further to justify their position.

Often they will take the form of a throwaway comment, such as "he's a big hitter, a serious player", or "it's a top job, lots of pressure", or "he brings in $200 million a year", or "he's got 500 people working for him." This chapter will look at all these arguments – both those openly expressed and those inferred from these casual remarks.

Money Motive

We have seen how Royal Dutch Shell awarded massive personal wealth to chief executive Jeroen van der Veer in 2008. The following year, as he was about to step down as chief executive, he made this intriguing comment: "You have to realise: if I had been paid 50 per cent more, I would not have done it better. If I had been paid 50 per cent less, then I would not have done it worse."

I have argued that Mr. van der Veer received this massive personal wealth because the company which happened to employ him operated in an environment that guaranteed huge revenue, and despite the fact that it failed to reach the minimum target of a series in which even the achievement of the maximum target would be hard to classify as exceptional. I have also argued that it would have been impossible, anyway, to attribute the company's success (or failure) to him as an individual.

And then we learn that, even according to himself, the level of financial reward had little or no bearing on van der Veer's own performance!

Is van der Veer an exception? Does financial incentive encourage people to work harder, arguably making high pay justified on the basis that it promotes high performance?

Not according to the 2007 Towers Perrin Global Workforce Study, which interviewed 90,000 employees in 18 countries and is trumpeted as the largest such workplace survey.

The study measured which factors attract employees to join a company, what motivates them once working there, and what persuades them to stay. "Competitive base pay" was indeed the prime reason why people joined a company. But it did not feature in the top ten reasons for wanting to leave a company. Nor did it feature in the top ten for "engagement", or motivation, when actually performing the job itself.

One could argue, of course, that most employees are not particularly interested in financial reward because they feel they cannot earn that much more anyway. A rival company might offer them a relatively substantial percentage increase in their salary in order to entice them, but once recruited, the prospects for further substantial salary increases are remote. And most employees will not receive annual bonuses based on performance.

Senior executives and many finance workers, one may suggest, are in a different category. Not only will they earn a large salary, but they also often stand to earn life-transforming additional money if their performance is deemed excellent, and often a very nice moderately life-changing consolation if their performance is deemed average or below. Surely that is all very motivating, despite what van der Veer claims? Surely they would want to work extremely hard to retain their job and the accompanying large salary, and if possible, obtain an extremely large bonus, rather than a smaller large one?

Executive Effort

Let's take the chief executive in a large public company first, and assume here that his influence on company performance is significant and that companies must therefore do everything in their power to ensure their maestro is highly motivated.

Perhaps we should begin with a couple of questions: Is the very highly-paid modern-day CEO more committed than chief executives pre-1980 before their salaries started shooting up? Is he more committed than the chief executive of a smaller company where pay will tend to be much lower?

We can't answer these questions one way or the other with any certainty. These three groups (modern-day CEOs of large public companies, their predecessors pre-1980 and small company CEOs) are likely to be, or to have been, highly motivated by comparison to most workers. How would you be able to distinguish between the three in terms of effort?

So, yet again, we are left to speculate. As van der Veer's comment implies, you can't try any harder than your utmost — there is a limit. Even if money is a major motivation for chief executives, we might suppose that an individual who appears ambitious and hard-working enough to be considered for the top position in a large public company would try just as hard in an attempt to earn, say, 30 times the pay of the average worker in the United States, as he would to earn 364 times, now the actual such ratio.

We might also suppose that an individual who seemed ambitious and hard-working enough to be considered for the top position pre-1980 expended just as much effort, once appointed, for much less money. And, finally, we might also suppose that a CEO of a small company, often its founder and owner, tries as hard as he possibly can to help to stave off the fierce competition that his company will usually face, competition no doubt considerably fiercer than that experienced by most large company CEOs.

We might also suggest that there will be other motivating factors which, together with a moderate financial incentive or perhaps even without any financial incentive, are likely to induce maximum effort from the large company CEO.

These factors might include the opportunity to make a personal impact (the will to make an impact is more important here than the eventual reality which, as we have seen, is often extremely difficult to establish); to perform interesting work; to assume a position of high status and some power and influence; to gain the respect of his peers; to see his ideas reach fruition; to make a name for himself. We should note that the President of the United States earns substantially less than most large company CEOs (the base salary is $400,000), and there is no shortage of able aspirants for this role.

Of course, one might say that if the chief executive's salary was to be reduced to the level of the President of the United States, both he and future aspirants would leave for a rival or enter an industry where the rewards are thought to be higher. And at this juncture, we come back, once more, to the talent ideology and reflect further on its pivotal role in maintaining high pay.

"The broader long-term risk of underpaying corporate executives", argue pay consultants Ira Kay and Steven van Putten, "is that top talent from colleges and business schools will enter other more lucrative, and arguably more interesting, professions, such as investment banking, venture capital, and management consulting. Private equity firms also recruit corporate executives for very lucrative pay packages. This puts upward pressure on corporate and CEO packages."

Herein lies the rub. Senior executives are not paid so much in order to motivate them, but in order to compete in the market for perceived talent. If we can motivate people to apply maximum effort for a lot less, we would only pay them a lot more if we believed that their ability to perform the job well is extremely rare and that to replace them would be a hugely onerous task. In my view, such a belief is ill-founded.

Financial Commitment

What about rewards for a top salesperson – a role in which his financial results are clearly measurable and transparent?

Few would dispute that a salesperson would perform better with some financial incentive than with none at all. The question is: how high is necessary to extract maximum effort? Can we say that a finance sector worker on a promise of a $1 million bonus would work harder than a pharmaceutical salesperson who stands to gain $50,000? Both, presumably, would normally be highly motivated, and it would be hard to differentiate their effort.

Again, the level of the incentive is not pitched to achieve maximum effort, but to compete in the market for perceived talent. If $50,000 was considered a good bonus in the finance sector as a whole, then employers in that sector would not worry so much that their "star" rainmakers would jump ship if offered that sum.

Indeed, the existence of proven excellent salespeople in other industries who work hard to achieve lower incentives should really act as a downward pressure on pay offered in the financial sector. If you can sell in one industry, there is no reason to think that you would not be able to sell in another. Once again, selling is a much rarer skill than the ability to acquire product or industry knowledge.

Financial incentives are often described as a good way of aligning the interests of the managers with those of the owners. They are said to counter the "principal-agent problem", which holds that employees might potentially work to further their own personal interests at the expense of shareholders.

If finance sector workers bring in revenue because they are highly motivated, the argument goes, the shareholders will be happy. If the chief executive is motivated to manage the company in a way that increases the profits and the value of the company, the shareholders will be happy. Interests, it is said, are properly aligned.

However, although incentives in themselves can help to ease the principal-agent problem, excessive incentives become part of the very same problem.

Some financial incentive might indeed serve to motivate a worker to pursue the interests of shareholders, but the talent ideology has artificially inflated such incentives for senior corporate executives and finance workers to an extreme level. These high-flying employees have devised and sustained a doctrine to earn themselves much more money when they do not really deserve it, a ruse clearly against the interests of the ultimate shareholders (you and me) who have to pay this money out.

Extremely high incentives are not simply a manifestation of this principal-agent problem. They may also threaten to multiply its negative effects. Incentives that offer the prospect of huge personal wealth increase the danger that the executive or employee will take risks that endanger the interests of shareholders, or merely skew targets (which are often very vague and open to interpretation anyway) and manipulate figures for their own benefit.

Hence, chief executives might be tempted to engineer a merger or acquisition, against the long-term interests of shareholders, in order to increase their pay. After all, chief executives of larger companies tend to be paid more, supposedly because they have to deal with greater "complexity", but in reality because there is more money around to pay themselves with.

Likewise, finance workers' incentives made it more likely that banks would engage in highly risky ventures. If your potential bonus is $50,000, you might shy away from high risk. You might get your $50,000 in the short term, but the long-term risk of losing your job as a consequence makes the venture seem unattractive.

But if your bonus is potentially several million, then the risk of losing your job is worth taking. As so many individuals within the finance sector were making this unconscious (or perhaps, sometimes, conscious) calculation, a culture of excessive risk-taking became deeply entrenched within the industry. It was this culture, created by the high rewards that are in turn shielded by the talent ideology, which was largely responsible for bringing the global financial system to its knees in 2008.

Siphoning Revenue

Recipients of high pay, and their allies, often argue that this pay is justified by the fact that the relevant individual was responsible for a far higher figure in revenue.

For example, a chief executive earning $20 million might be said to be well worth the money on the basis that his performance allegedly led to increases in profits and company value that far outweighed his compensation. Or a manager in a finance company earning $5 million might be said to deserve his pay because his department generated, say, $100 million worth of revenue. As we have seen,

50 per cent of investment banking revenue has traditionally been allotted to salaries and bonuses.

Let's sift through this argument. According to a 2008 report, the average grocery supermarket in the United States owned by a large chain generates $14 million in annual revenue. The average revenue per employee was $150,000.

There is a downward pressure on supermarket wages. The reason why average salaries in the average American grocery supermarket will be nowhere near even $75,000 (50 per cent of $150,000) is that the skills necessary to operate a till or stack shelves are regarded as very common.

It is not enough, therefore, to say an individual deserves a high salary just because the company, department or store he works for has generated a significant amount of revenue. That money can also go to the shareholders. One must also say that his contribution to the success is measurable, at least to a significant degree, and that the skills he brings to the job are extremely rare. There is no automatic relationship between revenue and pay.

It is true that there has to be high revenue to pay people high salaries in the first place. For example, the top European soccer players of the 1970s earned a fraction of what their counterparts in the modern era now earn, despite also possessing rare and highly measurable talent.

Why? Because the soccer industry now generates much more revenue than it did then due to much more lucrative sponsorship and television deals, and also arguably because there has been a growing appreciation of the rarity and impact of top players' talent (the ratio of wages to turnover in English soccer's top tier has also increased, from just over 50 per cent in the 1970s and 1980s, to 62 per cent in 2008, thus possibly supporting the argument that their talent is now valued even more highly). If these soccer players of yesteryear had been around today, they too would be looking forward to a life of supreme wealth and luxury.

As revenue has gone up in the soccer industry, the players have demanded more and the owners have concluded that they have little choice but to give in.

We have seen how the rewards handed to investment bankers have gone up and down with the vagaries of the economy and the money available in the industry. We have seen that Goldman Sachs set aside more than $11 billion for employee pay in the first half of 2009. David Viniar, the company's chief financial officer, defended such high pay. "We have a pay-for-performance culture," he said. "As you saw in 08, if we don't perform well, compensation goes down, and if we do, we reward people appropriately."

We often hear this refrain: "Why shouldn't a banker earn a $2 million bonus if he brought in $20 million of business?" The question is asked as if it would be mean and unfair to reject the request. But several questions need to be asked in return.

What does "brought in" mean? How many other people were involved in "bringing in" the business? Can we attribute that revenue specifically to that person? Would that banker have "brought in" $20 million of revenue if he had been working on his own, or for a company relatively unknown in the marketplace? How important was the role of the company's brand, which existed long before the banker joined the company, in "bringing in" the business?

Can we reasonably conclude that this business would still have arrived at the company if that banker had been run over by a bus five years ago? Precisely what skills were required by the banker to "bring in" this business? Can we make a convincing case that these skills are uncommon? Could, in fact, many other people be trained to acquire these skills? Could other people who have these skills but no easily attained specific industry knowledge have also potentially brought in $20 million of business if armed with this industry knowledge?

If all those questions are answered satisfactorily, then we can put up our hands. Yes, the banker deserves to earn his $2 million bonus and become wealthy, and the owners of the company have no choice but to become $2 million poorer. If they are answered unsatisfactorily, then we can say that shareholders have been duped (willingly or otherwise) into parting with money that by rights belongs to them.

"He deserves $x because he/his team/department/company generated $x of revenue" is a statement that makes no sense by itself. High revenue is a necessary reason for high pay, but not a sufficient one. An individual's claim to deserve a significant proportion of this revenue rests, once again, on the talent ideology.

Rolodex Power

Another argument used to defend high pay centres on the number and strength of an individual's contacts in the relevant marketplace. As the business writer Tom Peters put it: "Your power is almost directly proportional to the thickness of your Rolodex, and the time you spend maintaining it."

Although such contacts will undoubtedly be a major advantage to the individual worker in, for example, searching for a new job, they will only be useful to the individual's employer if he or she uses them to attract or retain business.

But in a large company, the commercial usefulness of individual personal contacts may be doubtful for several reasons. First, when a company sells a product or a service, there is a good chance that its strong brand and reputation figured prominently in the buyer's thought process. The product or service itself is also likely to be very well-known, and tested in the marketplace. Familiarity, trustworthiness and likeability of the salespeople may therefore be secondary to the buyer. Indeed, the buyer will frequently come to them without any attempted selling at all.

Second, the buyer may assume that the individual salesperson or account handler is typical of anyone that the large company would employ. In other words, their view of the company brand will determine, to a large extent, their judgment of the individual, no matter who he or she is. They also know they can ask at any point for that person to be removed from handling the account if they so wished, and replaced by someone they deemed more suitable.

Third, many people are likely to be involved in a major deal or account. When a large management consultancy firm like Accenture sells a major consulting contract to a big corporation like, say, Procter & Gamble, it is unlikely to be down to a single individual.

If a single crucial dealmaker or account manager is thought to be responsible, he might be said to have won the account because the client company deemed him reliable, hard-working and organised – worthy traits, but relatively common and eminently replaceable all the same. Indeed, it is unlikely that someone wins an account for that reason; his counterparts at competitor companies are also likely to be deemed reliable, hard-working and organised.

Perhaps he is a friend of the decision-makers at the client company, and therefore not easily replaceable. He would then deserve his bonus. But such relations also carry risks to his employer. For as long as the friendly decision-maker remains at the client company, the salesman can threaten to join a rival organisation, and take his loyal client with him. It's not a stable, or even necessarily profitable, situation for an employer to be in, especially if the well-connected salesman guards his friendship by blocking other channels of business with the client in question.

But will management even attempt to confront this problem? If a manager himself controls a high-earning account, he may well be loath to counter this culture of individual account ownership by forcefully instituting a more team-based client liaison. High pay for contacts therefore leaves shareholders vulnerable, once more, to the principal-agent problem, as well-positioned employees engineer a system in which they appropriate large sums of money on its route from client to shareholder.

The Cart or the Horse?

Some may say that it is not the personal contacts per se that attracts business. "Rainmakers", employees in the finance sector who are said to create significant new business and are rewarded with massive wealth as a result, rely principally on their reputation in the marketplace – their personal brand within the small world in which they operate.

We are not talking here of the many intelligent, reliable, hard-working, competent, personable employees who have built up their reputation over many years of performing similar work, but rather people who apparently possess an aura, presumably emanating from rare qualities, which then naturally attracts clients to the company.

Unfortunately, it's not clear what the substance of this aura involves. Perhaps the rainmaker has "put deals together" before, and this experience built his reputation. But what precisely were the rare personal qualities that enabled him to put these deals together? Indeed, couldn't we claim that anyone promoted to a senior position within a top investment bank, with its glowing brand, will automatically assume a powerful personal reputation that then attracts business?

Wouldn't anyone appointed to a senior position at Goldman Sachs, for example, be regarded as a "heavy hitter", provided that he appeared reasonably intelligent and confident, as many people do, not least when they are promoted to a senior position at a top investment bank?

Perhaps, indeed, we have got it the wrong way round once more. What if it isn't the abilities of the rainmaker that attract the business, but the substantial revenue inevitably attracted by someone in a prestigious position in a top investment bank that lull us into investing that person with supreme abilities. The false perception of these supreme abilities then results in the tag of "rainmaker".

Entrepreneurs, especially those who create a new industry or radically change an industry, could be more accurately described as rainmakers.

But as their individual contribution is obvious, maybe they don't feel the need to dress themselves in the vocabulary of mythology. For those currently labelled "rainmakers" in the finance industry, perhaps the better description would be "rain-collectors where it rains a lot".

Interestingly, the term "rainmaker", which denotes a magical power, is rarely used about people in other industries outside finance, where rewards just so happen to be much lower. But in the finance industry itself, the legend has served to make well-positioned individuals extremely rich.

The Pay Mirage

Rather than rare talent producing excellent results, and therefore staking a claim to high pay, the reverse would appear to be equally plausible: that high pay merely suggests rare talent, and provides a spurious explanation for good company performance.

Sounds far fetched? Academics Rachel Hayes and Scott Schaefer argue that companies might be inclined to raise the pay of their chief executives because they want investors to believe that the company has an above-average CEO. They named this theory the Lake Wobegon effect, after the author Garrison Keillor's fictional hometown in which all children are above average.

They point out that higher pay is seen as proof of higher ability. "Everyone knows that in well-functioning labour markets, better performers earn higher salaries," Schaefer says. If a company pays the CEO a comparatively low salary, analysts might conclude that he is not up the mark and will downgrade the firm's stock.

If, on the other hand, the company boosts the salary significantly, investors might conclude that the CEO is a superstar, and the stock price might jump. If the increase in the stock price is greater than the increase in the CEO's salary, then this could be a wise move by the firm. This logic could act as an upward pressure on executive pay, as all companies vie to pay their CEO more than the average.

It may well be the case, in Schaefer's words, that "in well-functioning labour markets, better performers earn higher salaries". But, at the top end, higher salaries may not actually relate to the recipient's superior ability – they simply coax us into thinking they do.

Return for Risk

Some claim that senior executives, and even finance workers, deserve their high pay because they accept substantial personal risk in their jobs. High pay presumably acts as compensation for this risk. Of all the increasingly desperate arguments used to defend high pay, this is surely the most ridiculous.

The alleged risk falls into three categories – reputation risk, career risk and financial risk. Countering the belief that top bankers have little to lose personally from undertaking risky corporate ventures, The (London) Times business editor David Wighton argued: "When Lehman went down, Dick Fuld, its chief executive, lost stock that a year earlier had been worth $700 million. He also lost for ever something he probably valued a great deal more — a reputation as a Titan of American business a lifetime in the making. Only an economist could think it was rational for someone to risk that."

The first point to make in response is that only the chief executive, and possibly one or two others, suffer an assault on their reputation when their company's fortunes plummet. Many very well-paid decision-makers just below the very top tier are not in public view, and their reputations do not suffer in a similar manner.

What's more, senior executives of major companies that perform disastrously, and who are subsequently heavily criticised in the media, often move on into other high-profile positions. For all but a tiny minority who are continuously and publicly disparaged, senior executives bear insignificant reputation risk and even less significant career risk.

Fuld has indeed become the fall-guy in the United States. He is publicly vilified and his reputation does indeed appear irrecoverable. In the UK, the same could be said of Sir Fred Goodwin, the former chief executive of Royal Bank of Scotland, a bank that had to be rescued by the government with effective nationalisation under his leadership, but still pays him a very large annual pension to say thank you.

But if we look at what has happened to others at the helm of rescued companies, we see that a tarnished reputation in no way inevitably sounds the death knell for a career.

For example, Stan O'Neal, of Merrill Lynch fame, was appointed a director of Alcoa, the aluminum company, in 2008. Andy Hornby, who led British bank HBOS to near-bankruptcy, was appointed as chief executive of Alliance Boots, the pharmacy retailer, in 2009. Daniel Mudd, the former head of bailed-out US mortgage lender Fannie Mae, was appointed as chief executive of investment company Fortress Investment Group, also in 2009.

Perhaps the subsequent employers of O'Neal, Hornby and Mudd believed, rightly, that their recruits could not be held personally responsible for the demise of their massive former companies. But one must then ask again: if they were not responsible for their companies' demise, why were they so handsomely rewarded when the same companies were making profits? They are either responsible for their company's fortunes, or they are not.

A number of recent management articles and books argue that it is very useful for senior executives to fail, because they can then learn from their failure. This is all great news for senior executives, and consequently for the consultants and academics who write articles and books in order to ingratiate themselves with them. A senior executive can succeed or fail, but the latter is merely a necessary step on the road to success. Heads I win, tails I win.

What about the CEO's financial risk? It is difficult to see that there is any at all. Stories of top executives receiving huge payoffs after poor company performance are legion. As we have seen, O'Neal received $162 million when he left Merrill. Wendelin Wiedeking, chief executive of Porsche, was awarded €50 million ($70 million) as a compensation package, and that after being paid €80 million ($112 million) in his final year.

Bob Nardelli, forced out as CEO of Home Depot in January 2007 after widespread criticism of poor stock performance and overall strategy, left with a severance package of $210 million. Not only did Nardelli edge O'Neal in the payoff stakes, he also reportedly earned $228 million in six years during his tenure, compared to O'Neal's $145 million in four full years (the latter having a slightly lower average).

To add insult to injury, he also finished one place higher in Portfolio Magazine's list of the worst CEOs of all time, at number 17. A matter of months after his departure from Home Depot, Nardelli was appointed chairman and chief executive of Chrysler.

At the top of the Porfotlio Magazine list of worst CEOs was Richard Fuld. Did Fuld, who joined Lehman Brothers in 1969 before embarking on a near forty-year career at the same company, take on huge personal financial risk, and deserve high pay in return when things were going well?

In his almost fifteen years as CEO, Fuld took home $466 million in total compensation. This figure includes base salary, bonus and long-term incentive plan payouts, and the value realised from stock option exercises and other benefits.

Wighton claims he still had $700 million worth of unexercised stock a year before Lehman's collapse. That may be true, but Lehman's stock price reached its all-time peak in 2007. The stock had been worth a lot less when he was given them. And the likelihood is that he was indeed given most or all of them, as opposed to buying them himself. In a hearing before a US Congress Committee, Fuld said that he received 85 per cent of his overall compensation in stock, and chose not to exercise much of this sum.

We can therefore look at Fuld's financial fate in another way. First of all, he was awarded huge pay, which was taken from shareholders and irrationally and undeservedly given to him. After all, how talented and irreplaceable could he have been if the company he led went bankrupt?

In addition, he was given company stock which was valued in 2007 at some $700 million. He told the committee: "I never sold my shares, and that's why I had 10 million left. I believed in this company. I could have sold that stock." We all make investment decisions with our cash, even if it is depositing it in our local bank, and we make a return based on the risk. Some we win, some we lose. Fuld's decision went wrong, like any can, but he still had whatever was left of $466 million to console him.

Claiming that Fuld's personal story represents one of genuine financial "risk" is a callous misappropriation of the term and an insult to real entrepreneurs who do genuinely put everything on the line – their house, their car, the lot – to support their own business. And indeed to shareholders who invested in Lehman with their own money and without receiving a massive salary from the company at the same time. The claim is also evidence of a naïve detachment from the real world of business, as opposed to the cushioned world of the high-flying corporate employee.

Besides, why should an individual be paid well simply for taking risk? You don't get entrepreneurs claiming that they deserve to be well-paid just because they have risked their principal possessions. To become wealthy, and to remain wealthy, their businesses must be continuously successful.

The presence of risk would only be a good argument for high pay if it was sufficient to deter all but a tiny few prospective candidates for a job with potentially substantial positive impact. As its effect on the supply of chief executive candidates is so infinitesimally negligible, the argument in this instance can be summarily dismissed as nonsense.

The Firing Line

What about those lower down the chain in finance companies? A common argument is that they deserve their high pay because they are in perpetual danger of being fired. Defending finance sector pay in 2007, Michael Snyder, policy chairman of the Corporation of London, the municipal governing body of the city's financial district, wrote: "The livelihoods (of City workers) are tied to the market in a way in which the rest of us would find chillingly risky. So risky that, as the worldwide credit crunch drags on, perhaps several thousand of those City "fat cats" could be losing their jobs."

Is Snyder suggesting that people on low pay do not lose their jobs in vast numbers in a recession? Any employee is always at risk from losing his or her job, and the more so when the economy falters. If they do lose their job, he or she does not generally have a large sum of money from past earnings to tide them through, unlike many finance workers.

When the economy picks up, the redundant finance worker is likely to find a way back within the same industry. The same could not be said for many lower-paid workers in industries such as mining and steel working that have experienced rapid decline in the developed world during the last few decades.

Once again, the threat of job insecurity should only be an argument for high pay if it was sufficient to deter all but a tiny few prospective candidates for a job with potentially substantial impact. How many graduates have turned down an opportunity to work in an investment bank because they think they might lose their job at some stage in the future?

Much is also made of high CEO turnover. But evidence suggests that a chief executive of a large company may, statistically, bear only marginally more job risk than the average worker. And as we have seen anyway, the failed large company CEO often receives a huge payout and cruises into another top job. Even if they don't, they will have enormous past earnings to draw on, not to mention a very large pension pot. Nardelli's estimated annual pension from Home Depot alone, for example, is $3.875 million.

There are those who argue that the bonus system in banks introduces personal risk. Criticising moves in some banks to increase bankers' salaries at the expense of bonuses, Hugo Dixon of the financial commentary website Breakingviews wrote: "One of the few good things about the old system of bankers' pay was that base salaries were pretty modest – meaning that there was scope for bankers to take a lot of the strain if their institutions fell on hard times."

One suspects that there are a good few businesspeople out there in the real world who would view such "modest" salaries, the "strain" of lower bonuses and zero financial commitment as an extremely easy and pampered working existence. There is no risk here whatsoever.

Some senior executives and finance workers in large companies may indeed engage each day in risky ventures. But we need to be scrupulous about what "risky" means in this context. This is corporate risk; their personal risk rarely rises above that of any other employee.

Hard Day's Night

The Occupational Outlook Handbook of the United States Department of Labor summarises the job of a "top executive" in three bullet points. One of them reads: "Top executives are among the highest paid workers; however, long hours, considerable travel, and intense pressure to succeed are common."

Note the juxtaposition here, as if the latter reality is a trade-off for the former reward. Indeed, we often hear high pay defended on the basis that the recipients work very hard and under great pressure.

Is this rational? One can certainly imagine that the chief executive of a large company devotes the vast majority of his waking hours, even at weekends, to company matters. They are also constantly under the spotlight of media and shareholder attention.

James Citrin, a senior consultant at Spencer Stuart, the executive search firm, surveyed 20 CEOs and "found that nineteen of them rose before 6 a.m. every day, with more than half up before 5:30". He also discovered that "almost all of them check their e-mail first thing upon waking up". Does this commitment deserve more money?

For a blue-collar worker, the hours spent on the job will often affect income. Overtime will result in more money. But a white-collar worker, particularly above a certain level, is often expected to spend as many hours as is necessary at their work. Their salary will be unaffected by the amount of time they put in. What determines their pay, or what should determine their pay, is their value to the company and how much it would cost to replace them with someone else of equal potential value.

The chief executive is certainly put under pressure to succeed. But so are lots of people. Does a surgeon, who will usually earn much less than a chief executive, experience pressure to succeed in an operation on a sick patient? One would expect so, when the alternative to success might be the patient's death. Does a zoo keeper, who will earn a lot less again, experience a pressure to succeed when entering a lion's cage to feed him? One would expect so, when the alternative to success might be his own death. Or how about the platoon leader taking his men into battle, where it's not just his own life but those of his men that are at risk from any slight error?

Blog comments by finance workers defending their income on the basis of high pressure and long hours are very common. Here is one such comment in response to an article in The New York Times: "Its high pressure, requiring long, long hours of risk assessment and nerves to take risks. Most folks don't like this type of arrangement and it's a 7 day a week job. The reward is a nice paycheck and the penalty is the door leading to the street!"

Once again, we see the naivety resulting from a cosseted working life. The writer may be unaware that underperformance in many much lower-paid jobs leads to the same door. I would also argue that many people (not everybody, not a large proportion, but many people) would in fact be prepared to work in such an environment for much less money and still be able to produce good results.

The high rewards in the finance sector are not based on the jobs themselves, but on the fact that the industry generates huge revenue which the employees can then grab before it gets to the shareholders.

The Golden Standard

A frequent explanation for the high pay of an individual chief executive is that it is based on the pay of his counterparts in the same industry or in a company of a similar size. He "deserves" $20 million because the CEO of a rival firm receives a comparable amount.

Such comparisons will inevitably speed up the increase in overall executive pay during a boom economy, and slow down the decrease when the economy deteriorates. Most companies seek to pay at least the median level, and more aim for the upper quartile than for the lower quartile. This is possibly because companies think investors might view a well-paid CEO as above average, as Hayes and Schaefer argue, and almost certainly also because they want their CEO to be "motivated".

Pay comparisons, informal or otherwise, take place at all levels of the job market. Say a secretary earning $40,000 goes to her manager and asks for a raise to $50,000. If the manager knows that he can get an equally proficient secretary for $35,000, he is unlikely to agree.

The problem with such comparisons comes when they perpetuate a level of pay that is irrational and unnecessarily penalises the shareholder. Whereas the labour market works effectively for the vast majority of jobs, those at the top have concocted the self-interested talent ideology to distort the labour market in which they themselves operate. Therefore, any comparison at this level by definition accepts the tenets of this ideology and sustains the high pay it has spawned.

If you accept the talent ideology, then there is of course no problem with pay comparisons at the top level. If you don't, then it is difficult to defend irrationally high pay for one job on the basis of others' irrationally high pay.

CHAPTER 5

Fame and Fortune

How many times have you heard someone say that top sports people, or leading movie stars, deserve what they earn because they need to be properly motivated, or because they work exceptionally hard, or because they work under great pressure, or because their reputation is at constant risk?

The probability is that you will have never heard anyone say this, and this is despite the fact that all these things are undoubtedly true.

To achieve genuine excellence in any pursuit, one has to be highly motivated and to work hard. In professional sport, this is transparently clear, as indeed everything always is in sport. Lazy players with great natural ability fall by the wayside. Committed players with less ability can sometimes win. One team will inflict a heavy defeat on another of apparently equal ability, and the losing coach will explain that his team was simply beaten by a more determined opposition. "All right Mister, let me tell you what winning means," the great American football coach, Vince Lombardi, once said. "You're willing to go longer, work harder, give more than anyone else."

Think indeed of the tremendous self-sacrifice, the iron self-discipline and the countless hours of monotonous practice involved in reaching the pinnacle of sport, ahead of all those millions who would dearly love to be in the same position.

What about pressure? The putt to win the Masters, the penalty to win the World Cup, the serve to save Championship point, and all in front of millions, if not billions of people. If you fail, all the sports journalists and armchair critics, from Los Angeles to Sydney, will queue up to label you a "loser", a person who may be blessed with talent but who just didn't have the temperament at the last gasp to grab the opportunity of a lifetime. No corporate scenario comes to mind that would even come close to that level of personal stress.

A movie star is riding the crest of a wave and is the subject of perpetual media attention. But her next film is an embarrassing flop. Her performance is ridiculed by the critics, and her career nosedives. In such a highly competitive environment, she may never fully recover. Every high-profile film entails substantial reputation risk for any successful actor.

If all these things are undoubtedly true, then why are they not used as justifications for high pay? For the same reason, I would suggest, that you can easily find out what a tennis player receives for winning a major tournament, or how much a top baseball player or soccer player earns every week, but you can't find out what a highly-paid individual trader in a major investment bank earns. And for the same reason that when different highly respected newspapers and research companies try to determine the total compensation of a large company CEO, they wade through the baffling, opaque figures to come up with wildly varying totals.

This is the reason: The sports star and movie celebrity does not suffer from the same deep-seated insecurity borne out of a lack of clear measurability of personal value. We therefore don't get the same scramble to defend high pay that we witness in the corporate world. Tortured justifications are simply unnecessary.

Nor do sports and movie stars have any reason to dissemble what they earn. They are not worried what others think, because they know that it would be difficult to build a rational, market-based argument against their income. That same confidence cannot be ascribed to high-fliers in the corporate world, whose earnings are either totally invisible, or enmeshed in complexity.

"After the compensation packages of star athletes are negotiated, clubs have little reason to try to camouflage the amount of pay and to channel pay through arrangements designed to make the pay less visible," write Lucian Bebchuk and Jesse Fried in their book "Pay without Performance". "While athletes are paid generously during the period of their contracts, clubs do not generally provide them with a large amount of compensation in the form of postretirement perks and payments. Clubs also generally do not provide athletes with complex deferred compensation arrangements that serve to obscure total pay." As the authors point out, these are common practices in the field of executive compensation.

The word "talent" is used in the boardrooms because it implies invaluable rarity, and triggers mental associations with great sports people, actors and musicians who have traditionally been considered as talented, and have reaped the resulting financial rewards.

"We are just like them," plead the corporate high-fliers. Stan O'Neal, we were urged to believe, is just like Tiger Woods. Jeroen van der Veer is just like Johan Cruyff. Vikram Pandit is just like Sachin Tendulkar.

But they are not like them at all.

The Lone Star

To recap the three necessary conditions for high pay. First, there obviously must be sufficient revenue available. Second, the recipient of high pay should be a key contributor to the pursuit of the organisation's objectives; he should make a measurable and substantial positive impact, or at least there should be a sound rational reason for believing that he will make a measurable and substantial positive impact in the future. Third, we need to demonstrate beyond reasonable doubt that his abilities are sufficiently rare to make him extremely difficult to replace.

Let's now use this framework to look at the pay of sports stars, sports coaches and celebrities, and then compare the conclusions to those we have already drawn for senior executives and finance workers.

The top-earning female athlete in the world from June 2007 to June 2008 was Maria Sharapova, the Russian tennis player, who earned $26 million in prize money and commercial endorsements. After she has paid her coaches and other expenses and taxes, there is no-one else around to lay claim to this money apart from her.

The argument about whether she makes a measurable impact or is replaceable is redundant, just as it is with the independent entrepreneur who owns his own business. Sharapova obviously makes an impact on her own success, and no-one else can be her apart from herself. (It's worth noting, as an aside, that the earnings of Sharapova, one of the world's best female tennis players who has entertained millions throughout the world, would not have placed her anywhere near the top of the pay rankings for US CEOs.)

Angelina Jolie, the highest-paid movie actress in the world in the period from June 2008 to June 2009, pipped Sharapova to earn annual income of $27 million for her participation in the films "Wanted" and "Salt". Again, after she has paid her agents' fees and other expenses, who else should get this money apart from her?

One could question whether tennis tournament chiefs and Hollywood studios were paying Sharapova and Jolie too little or too much. But think of these two women as businesses, not individuals. This book does not attempt to question how much Shell charges its customers for oil, but only why the company's chief executive should become rich on the resulting revenue. As Sharapova and Jolie are their own businesses, their profit can only go to one person – themselves.

Many employee sports stars also make a great deal of money from endorsing products sold by major corporations. For example, the cricketer with the highest income in the world in 2009 was the captain of the India national team, Mahendra Singh Dhoni. Out of the $10 million he received in the previous year, $8 million was reportedly from commercial endorsements, for such companies as Reebok and Pepsi.

Dhoni earned this $8 million through the power of his own brand, acting as his own business in other words. Questioning his own impact on this income, and judging his replaceability as a private businessman, is again clearly nonsensical.

It is, however, when revenue has to be divided up among employees that we can reasonably challenge, on market grounds, how much someone is paid. So it is to top-earning sports people and television celebrities who receive the bulk of their income as employees of their club or company that we now turn.

Deep Pockets

The first condition for high pay is that there is sufficient money available in the industry. In some team sports, excellence as a player doesn't inevitably lead to wealth; there simply isn't the money around to allow it.

Lacrosse, a team game of native American origin, is very much a minority sport in North America. In 2009, average attendance for Major League Lacrosse (the six-team professional outdoor league) was just 5,557, a mere fraction of the crowds drawn by baseball or American football, let alone of their huge television audiences.

As a result of its minority status, even top performers such as Paul Rabil of the Boston Cannons, the league's Most Valuable Player (MVP) for 2009, are reputed to earn no more than $20-30,000 per year. The story might be somewhat different if Rabil was equivalently adept at baseball or American football, or if lacrosse started to generate similar levels of interest.

Indeed, before money started pouring into English professional soccer in the 1990s through lucrative television contracts and more professional merchandising, successful players traditionally squirreled just enough money away to buy a pub or some other small business to manage after retirement from the game. Others ended up in poverty.

Larry Lloyd, a member of the Nottingham Forest team that won the European Cup in 1979 and 1980, is one of several players from that era to have sold their winners' medals, receiving a mere £12,000 ($20,400) for his in 2001. "Selling my European medals is the greatest regret of my life," Lloyd later recalled. 'I feel sick when I think about it. But needs must when the devil drives and the devil was certainly at the wheel then." Lloyd will have been earning only around £15,000 ($25,500) a year during his peak years as a player, a pittance compared to modern-day salaries.

Personal Impact

Just because there is a large amount of money available in the organisation or industry, it doesn't necessarily follow that workers should be paid a huge amount of money. First of all, their positive impact has to be measurable and substantial as well.

The primary objective of the sports team is to win games and championships. Indeed, many owners of sports clubs are focused on the profit of the organisation, which itself derives largely from on-field success, but there are others that seem not to care too much. For example, some extremely wealthy owners of European soccer clubs appear more interested in the enjoyment, status and possible championship-winning success conferred by ownership, rather than in the financial rewards this may generate.

The sports team will rely more or less solely for its success in winning games on the individual and collective contribution of its members in relation to that in rival teams. What other explanation can there be? Maybe, in some relatively rare instances, a slice of luck beyond the team's control may work in its favour when a mistaken decision of the umpire/referee decides the game.

Individual impact on this team success varies to some extent according to the sport. In certain games, such as baseball or cricket, one player's performance is more or less unaffected by the quality of his colleagues. The individual's value to the team is therefore extremely clear, and will tend not to fluctuate too much even if the player in question switches to a poorer team. In these sports, the team's performance will approximate the sum of individual contributions.

Sachin Tendulkar, the Indian batsman, has scored more runs than anyone else in the history of Test match cricket. The Indian national team has been one of the best in the world throughout his career. Even if he had been playing for one of the worst, say Bangladesh, there is no reason to think that his individual performance would have been appreciably worse.

He would undoubtedly have been adversely affected by the low morale of a losing team, by the greater pressure involved in attempting to hold a team together single-handedly and by a shortage of able batting partners. But his performances would still have been excellent, if not quite as excellent, and made a huge positive impact on the team.

However, in more interactive sports, such as basketball and soccer, a top player may well suffer a greater drop in fortunes when playing in a poor team, or even perhaps in a team whose style doesn't suit his own, thus markedly hindering his ability to make an equivalent contribution. Overall team performance in these sports appears to result from a complex combination of individual ability and collective cohesiveness.

Many pundits believe that George Best was the greatest British soccer player of all time. With his outstanding talent, he helped Manchester United to win the European Cup in 1968, and scored 137 goals in only 361 games for them. His skills, however, were not enough to help his comparatively poor national team, Northern Ireland, even to qualify for a major tournament, let alone win one.

We can speculate that Best's presence would have improved the Northern Ireland soccer team considerably, but not by as much as

Tendulkar would have improved the Bangladesh cricket team.

Rugby and American football provide something of a half-way point. Players in certain roles depend very heavily on the assistance of team-mates, as in basketball and soccer, while others are more self-reliant.

An MIT Sloan Management Review article from 2008 looked at how well star American footballers performed once they switched teams. The authors found that the measurable performance of wide receivers, whose play is "governed by complex interactions with colleagues", tended to decline markedly in the year after switching clubs, before recovering. On the other hand, the performances of punters, whose ability to kick a ball "is almost entirely dependent on the individual's strength and skill", remained constant after switching.

Despite pausing to recognise this variation between sports, we can still make the general observation that individual contribution to team success in sport is highly, if not perfectly, measurable. From this we can make a rational judgement that a top player will greatly improve the overall performance of his team. This is true for all sports, but is more true for some than others.

Like for Like

Measurable positive impact alone doesn't necessitate high pay. It must also be extremely difficult to replace the individual concerned.

In the opening chapter, we discussed the talent of Lionel Messi, the Argentinean soccer star. Another example is the baseball player Alex Rodriguez, nicknamed A-Rod. In late 2007, he signed a contract worth $275 million with his club, the New York Yankees, to be paid over ten years in unequal instalments (the highest being $32 million in 2009), and with a reported incentive package that could raise the total value as high as $305 million. The Rodriguez contract was by far the largest in baseball history, eclipsing his own record set when he signed a ten-year contract worth $252 million with the Texas Rangers before the 2001 season.

Was he worth it? Let's look at some of A-Rod's achievements. At the age of 32 years and 8 days, he became the youngest player ever to hit 500 home runs, breaking a record set just under seven decades previously, in 1939. He has scored more runs than anybody in an American League season five times. He has won the award of Most Valuable Player (MVP) for an American League season three times.

Despite his outstanding record, Rodriguez has come in for criticism, chiefly emanating from a perception that his teams fared better after he left, and that he sometimes doesn't perform his best in tense, critical ("clutch") situations. Both criticisms have nevertheless been hotly contested, and were largely dispelled by his excellent performance and six home runs in the Yankees' World Series victory in 2009. He has also admitted to the use of performance-enhancing drugs between 2001 and 2003, a revelation that inevitably tarnished his professional reputation.

On the other hand, many assert confidently that Rodriguez is simply one of the greatest baseball players of all time. Could Rodriguez have been adequately replaced at any stage in his illustrious career with an equally powerful hitter whose teams have won more World Series championships, who performs more consistently than he has done "in the clutch", and whose professional reputation is whiter than white? Although some current players may be able to claim that they fulfil one or two of these conditions, none can to all. If not beyond all doubt absolutely unique, A-Rod's talent can confidently be labelled as extremely rare.

From the perspective of his employers at the onset of his contract, offering him extremely high pay appears to have been rational. There was enough money in the respective organisations to pay him and his former performance had been clearly excellent. Although, like any top sportsmen, he may have had slight deficiencies in his game, it would have been extremely difficult to identify a similar player more likely to help the team to success.

Sports Stars, Chief Executives and Finance Workers

How do the impact and replaceability of sports stars measure up against those of chief executives of large public companies?

Whereas there are persuasive alternative explanations for corporate success that do not relate to human ability, no sports team has ever won a championship because the economy is strong, or because it operates in an uncompetitive oligopoly, or because it represents a brand that is popular.

In other words, while Shell's performance in 2008 and previous years may have had little to do with the performance of van der Veer and his senior management team, Inter Milan will have won the Italian league soccer championship for four consecutive years from 2006 solely because of the performance of its team, and the individuals within that team.

What about replaceability? Inside the company itself, there will likely be anything from several dozen to several hundred experienced executives who are sufficiently able, competent, intelligent, well-educated, industrious, robust and dependable to appear convincing in the CEO role. The impressive rank of "chief executive" does have a knack of making people appear more confident and convincing anyway, perhaps because they become accustomed to others agreeing with them more.

Outside the company, there will be a similar number of candidates multiplied by the number of rivals in the industry. That is, of course, if you confine your search to the same industry; there is no reason to assume that intelligent, well-educated people should not learn the necessary information about a completely new industry. If they are graduates, they will have mastered Aristotle or astrophysics or some such at one stage in their lives, so some of them might just about be up to this task.

We should also mention the complete outsider. We don't know for sure that an excellent head teacher, or head of a charity, or consultant surgeon, or top lawyer wouldn't make a very competent chief executive within a short space of time. How would we know, when they have never tried to be? Anyway, can anyone identify which necessary skills they won't possess?

By contrast, hardly anyone within baseball and absolutely no-one from outside it could feasibly have replaced Rodriguez, for instance.

What about the highly-paid finance worker in comparison to the sports star? John Varley, chief executive of Barclays, is one of many to suggest that the two groups bear striking similarities.

"The football analogy certainly goes some way I think [to explain bonuses] ... There is simply no higher priority than to ensure we field the very best people. That in a sense is exactly the same as a football manager if they are going to win. Our obligation is to ensure we pay appropriately."

Unlike with the sports team, there are several external factors influencing the performance of the finance team. The power of the brand, long predating the arrival of its "star" employees, will very likely influence the team's revenue. So, certainly, will the strength of the economy. And so will a very large element of luck, manifested perhaps in sudden demand for its products or services that are triggered by events beyond the team's control, or in the performance of its market trades, where luck may play a major role.

It could, in fact, be that the advantage gained by the quality of the finance team's people is very minimal, but we can't say that for sure. So then we ask: how easily replaceable are the highest-paid members of a finance team in comparison to someone like Messi or Rodriguez?

Many people – not everybody, not the majority, not even a large minority, but many people – may well have the ability to sell a product, or to construct a complex deal, or to gain short-term returns on an investment. Precisely what skills are involved that are so staggeringly scarce? Many others sell products, make successful short-term decisions and construct complex deals in other industries for much less money.

Nevertheless, we could say, as far as the "rainmaker" is concerned, that it is not his talent per se that attracts business, but his reputation in the marketplace. But the talent ideology is still at play here. This reputation will often itself result from the false perception that he does indeed possess rare talent.

We can also suggest that his reputation may owe a great deal to the brand of the company he represents and the status of the position he occupies, and that a replacement in the same role in the same company may quickly engender a similar reputation.

In other words, we can't safely disassociate the reputation of the rainmaker from the reputation of the company he works for, or has worked for. In fact, the former may completely depend on the latter. But it is unlikely that there would have been anyone in the entire world who could have built a similar reputation to Messi or Rodriguez if they had replaced them, no matter how powerful the brand of Barcelona or the New York Yankees.

The Team Coach

If the high pay of sports stars is rational, what about the pay of their boss, the coach? His apparent success may conceivably owe more to the quality of his players, than to his own coaching. He may by chance have inherited an excellent group of players, or a sufficiently extensive budget to recruit an excellent group of players.

Also his skills appear more replaceable: the ability to recruit, organise and motivate a highly-paid group of young players and consistently adopt match-winning tactics may well be uncommon, but they seem much less obviously rare than the ability to play sport at the highest level.

How do we know, for example, that a top coach from a different sport wouldn't excel with the same group of players? Or a proven coach from lower down the league, or an excellent amateur coach, or maybe even an excellent people manager from the business world who is a fan of the sport in his spare time? Although we may argue, for instance, that players may respond less well to coaches without proven success at the highest level in their sport, we don't know this for sure, and we don't know for sure that this lack of faith in the coach would have a detrimental effect on team performance.

With their impact and replaceability both debatable, high pay for coaches seems less rational than high pay for players. And that impression is reflected in the reality.

Phil Jackson, the coach of the Los Angeles Lakers basketball team who has led teams to a record ten NBA titles, was reported in 2009 to earn an annual salary of $10.3 million, whereas his star player, Kobe Bryant, earns just over $23 million.

Terry Francona, who led the Boston Red Sox to two World Series championships in four years after an 86-year wait, has a contract worth on average $4 million a year. Thirteen players on the team's roster earned more than him in 2009 (there are nine players in a baseball team).

In September 2009, Lionel Messi signed a contract worth €10.5 million a year after taxes ($14.7 million), whereas Pep Guardiola, his coach who led Barcelona to a treble of trophies during 2009 (a feat unprecedented for a Spanish team), earned a total of €4 million ($5.6 million) during that year.

The Coach and the Chief Executive

But although the top coach's impact and replaceability are open to question, there are still persuasive reasons for thinking that the high pay of a top coach is substantially more rational than that of a chief executive of a major public company.

First, his pay is less easily attributable to pure status, and therefore more to ability and performance. Aside from the finance industry, the chief executive will almost certainly be paid more (often a great deal more) than anyone else in the organisation, for the simple reason that he is at the top. On the other hand, a coach tends to earn less than his star players.

Second, the coach runs a much smaller organisation than the CEO. Someone in charge of a squad of twenty or thirty people is much more likely to exert an influence on the average level of individual employee performance than someone at the head of a company of 50,000.

In the latter case, there will be many other people lower down the company who will also have some, and probably greater, influence on such performance. What's more, the performance of any one individual player in a sports team is likely to be much more crucial to organisational success than the performance of any one individual employee in a massive company.

Third, and following on from this point, the coach is likely to be a major factor in the star player agreeing to join a team, and certainly agreeing to stay with it. And, once again, the star player in a small sports team is much more likely to affect overall performance than any employee within a large corporate organisation, whose contact with the chief executive may well be extremely distant anyway.

Many surveys point to the important role of the immediate supervisor in employee commitment and retention. One extensive Gallup survey, with more than a million employee respondents from a broad range of industries and countries, concluded as follows: "The talented (sic) employee may join a company because of its charismatic leaders, its generous benefits and its world class training programs, but how long that employee stays and how productive he is while he is there is determined by his relationship with his immediate supervisor."

If the player's relationship with his coach is fraught, he may well be tempted by offers of equal or slightly higher pay from elsewhere, with a potentially very harmful effect on team performance. (Indeed, the biographies of the most successful coaches are littered with examples of star player loyalty to them.) The coach also often decides, or has an important role in deciding, which particular star players the club should recruit that will best gel within the overall team unit, or which youngsters the club should recruit that may potentially be stars one day.

In both these senses, the coach appears pivotal to team success.

Fourth, the large company's success may well rely almost totally on factors that have little to do with the contribution of its chief executive, such as a booming economy. On the other hand, the performance of the team of players is more or less the only reason for a sports team's success. And the coach manages the team. Even if you believe that his impact is minimal (which I don't), he is still competing with far fewer other possible success factors than the chief executive.

Fifth, we can speculate with some confidence that the top coach is generally better at his job than the chief executive is at his. The coach will usually only be appointed to a top position when he has led other teams to success as a coach. But, once again, even the chief executives who owe their appointment to apparent success as a chief executive elsewhere may well have had extremely little to do with that success.

Besides, as we have seen, most newly appointed chief executives in major global companies are appointed from inside the same organisation, and therefore will have had no previous experience as chief executive whatsoever.

The first-time CEO will owe his rise to the top to factors that are often not pertinent to his potential in his new job - how much he is liked or noticed by those above him in the hierarchy; his skill at self-promotion and internal politics; his apparent success in managing a department whose success will in fact inevitably owe a great deal to a whole range of reasons that have nothing to do with him; and, finally, his own performance in a functional (i.e. completely non-managerial) role.

On that final point, many successful sports coaches would never have had the chance to become successful if their playing career had been taken into account. At the start of the 2008-9 season in the English premiership, none of the coaches of the top four teams from the previous year had represented their respective countries at international level when they were players.

As Arrigo Sacchi, the successful Italian soccer coach who himself never made the grade as a player, once put it: "You don't have to have been a horse to be a good jockey." Doing a job, running an organisation, and managing people doing a job, are all completely different roles; a lesson that professional sport has mostly grasped, but the corporate world appears yet to understand, often promoting people to more senior positions simply because they appear to be good at doing something completely different.

Despite these five reasons for leading one to think that the high pay of a coach is substantially more rational than the high pay of a chief executive, the latter is paid far more. According to the research firm Equilar, the average total earnings for a large company chief executive in the United States in 2008 was $10.8 million,half a million more than the very highest-paid sports coach in the US, Phil Jackson.

Of course, large companies will have much greater revenue than sports clubs. But that should potentially translate into better returns for the shareholders, not massive wealth for senior management.

Celebrity Value

We have seen that the talent of top sports stars is both clearly valuable and extremely difficult to replace. Many people may not like the thought of sometimes uneducated, boorish young men earning huge amounts of money - opinion polls in the UK, for instance, reveal that people believe soccer players to be overpaid – but the fact that their employers do pay them so much is, in fact, entirely rational.

Outside the world of sport, however, highly-paid celebrities in the entertainment industry possess an ability that is much less easily measurable, and therefore much less obviously rare. So are their employers overpaying them?

Let's take as an example Katie Couric, the highest-paid news show anchor in the United States in 2009. In 2006, after 15 years as the co-presenter of "Today", the NBC's breakfast news show, she signed a five-year contract with CBS to be the anchor of "CBS Evening News". In doing so, she became the first woman to act as regular solo host of a major network evening news show. Her new annual salary was reported to be $15 million, a figure very similar to her reported previous earnings at NBC.

CBS chiefs believed that Couric could rescue their evening show's ratings that had mostly been lagging at third place behind their rival shows broadcast at NBC and ABC, whose own figures had themselves been declining in an overall trend caused primarily, it is widely thought, by the rise of the internet. It was felt that she would be particularly effective at attracting women and younger viewers to the show.

Good-looking and with an easy manner, Couric had demonstrated her popularity at "Today", a show that consistently achieved high viewing figures and where she earned the media sobriquet of "America's sweetheart". When she filled in for Jay Leno for one night in 2003 as the host of "The Tonight Show", the viewing figures rose by a whopping 42 per cent. Celebrity websites and magazines regularly feature stories about Couric's personal life, with many people seemingly eager to register their comments explaining why they like or dislike her.

Whatever the eventual results of their strategy (they were decidedly mixed in the first three years), the decision of CBS executives to offer Couric such a high salary was entirely rational.

She was already earning a similar salary, so to entice her they presumably had to offer at least the same. The profits for the show depend on advertising income, which itself depended on the shows' ability to attract the affluent and therefore highly sought-after 25-54 age group. The popularity of the show relies, at least to some extent, on the popularity of its presenters. And Couric had proven popularity. Her potential positive impact, in other words, could at the time of her appointment be rationally perceived as substantial.

However, it was not talent that made her potential impact substantial, but her celebrity. Women sufficiently good-looking, personable, intelligent, hard-working and articulate to be considered as a news show host are not nearly as rare as an annual salary of $15 million might suggest. Many women – not all women, not the majority, not even a large minority, but many women – would qualify.

But almost all such women are not known widely. As the academic Moshe Adler has argued, there may be a considerable number of people with sufficient ability to achieve stardom in the entertainment industry. But audiences want attention to be focused on only one or two, so they can derive enjoyment from talking about them with others and from reading about them in publications about famous people.

These one or two, by sheer chance, then become wealthy and famous, with similarly able people left only to rue their luck and seek less exciting career avenues. They deserve high pay for the same reason that people who win the lottery deserve their winnings. They got lucky, so good luck to them!

There may well be other Katie Couric's out there working as doctors or marketing executives or bringing up children, just as there may well be other Tom Cruises out there waiting tables while acting in local amateur theatre. But that doesn't matter when employers come to decide stars' pay, which, unlike in sport, is based principally on their ability to attract audiences, not their ability per se. And no-else can be Katie Couric or Tom Cruise apart from themselves. They are, in that sense, irreplaceable.

(Even in sport, celebrity, rather than talent, can occasionally supply the main reason for extremely high pay, and more often may arguably add a supplement to earnings. Soccer team LA Galaxy's recruitment in 2007 of the ageing but famous David Beckham, who takes a proportion of the club's ticket and merchandise sales, is a clear example of the former. Recent studies of Italian and Spanish soccer argue that public notoriety does indeed result in higher earnings for players than their talent alone would warrant.)

Some have criticised Couric's appointment at CBS by saying that she lacks the necessary gravitas to present "hard news" of national and international significance, and interview major political personalities on an evening news show, being more suited to the softer style of a breakfast show with its regular gossip and cookery features.

But even if that were true, and her highly-regarded interview with vice-presidential candidate Sarah Palin in 2008 and prestigious awards for her show appear to indicate otherwise, it would by no means suggest that CBS's decision to pay her more than any other news anchor was irrational. She may have had to be considered by her prospective employers to be good enough as a "hard news" presenter, a skill that a considerable number of American journalists can claim to possess, but she was first and foremost selected for her celebrity.

One could say, of course, that the highly-paid chief executive or finance worker also trades on his reputation. But such a reputation in a given marketplace is not the same as celebrity. Whereas the celebrity relies on little more than celebrity itself, the reputation of the highly-paid corporate worker will depend on a perception of having a rare talent to do a specific job, which is very likely to be false. Moreover, whereas the celebrity relies solely on his or her name, the reputation of the highly-paid corporate worker may well depend to a large extent on the brand of the company for which he works, or has worked.

Peas from Different Pods

The high pay of sports stars and celebrities is much more rational than that of chief executives and finance workers. But how do we explain why one set of employers would arrive at a rational decision, and another set at an irrational one?

Let's start at the beginning. If large companies are indeed paying their senior executives much more than is necessary, and if finance sector companies are indeed paying a significant chunk of their workforce much more than is necessary, then we can explain this outcome in two very different ways.

We might suggest that the people who recommend, award, rubberstamp and support such high pay are making a genuine commercial miscalculation. Or we might suggest that they themselves benefit from the same culture of high pay, are keen to perpetuate it, and are certainly loath to endanger it.

In my view, the latter is true. They have devised the false and empty talent ideology, use highly dubious and increasingly desperate other arguments to defend their pay, and go out of their way to obscure its real level. If high pay was an honest miscalculation, why would they have gone to so much trouble? They protest too much – as with the Player Queen in "Hamlet", they reveal their dishonesties by the extent of their efforts to conceal them.

On the other hand, if sports clubs and television companies are paying their star performers much more than is necessary, there is only one very likely explanation. They would have made a genuine miscalculation.

The people who make the decisions to award high pay in these organisations cannot benefit personally from such overpayment. This is true if they are the owners or shareholders, and this is true if they are managers operating on behalf of owners or shareholders.

Private owners of sports clubs and television stations want to keep as much money for themselves as possible. Why would they benefit personally from paying their employees more than is necessary?

Of course, the same could be said of private owners of companies that trade within the knowledge economy in the corporate world. But the managers who operate these companies on behalf of owners have a personal interest in duping them about the value and indispensability of top employees. Once again, this is a facet of the principal-agent problem, which holds that employees might potentially work to further their own personal interests at the expense of the owners.

The principal-agent problem, on the other hand, cannot have any influence on the pay of sports stars and celebrities. The dynamic is very different. Managers of sports clubs and television companies are white-collar office workers, not sports stars or celebrities. If, say, the value of Wayne Rooney, the star Manchester United soccer player, is artificially exaggerated and his pay inflated as a result, then David Gill, the United chief executive, does not stand to gain personally in any way.

Gill will relate his pay to that of those beneath him within the managerial structure of the organisation, and to that of other chief executives of similar organisations, not to that of Rooney, who operates in a wholly separate field. And it is a good job for Gill that he won't compare himself to top footballers. His annual pay was estimated at £1.48 million in 2008 ($2.5 million), whereas Rooney's basic salary before bonuses (and independent commercial revenue through private sponsorship) was estimated to be £6 million ($10.2 million) around this time.

If Gill recommends to the owners of the club, the Florida-based Glazer family, that Rooney has to be paid very well in order to retain his services, this would have no indirect effect on his own income – except insofar as Rooney's extremely rare talent results in more revenue for the organisation as a whole, which is a rational commercial reason for high pay. But if Gill recommends that someone beneath him in the executive structure should be paid extremely well because of the huge potential difficulty in replacing them, then he is supporting the white-collar talent ideology from which he himself benefits.

Even if Gill overpays Alex Ferguson, the Manchester United coach, then he does not stand to gain personally in any way. Gill occupies a wholly different sphere of work from Ferguson, and their respective levels of pay will therefore be completely unrelated.

(In an investment bank, a "star" trader will often earn more than the executive who has recommended and awarded his salary. However, the principal-agent problem is still relevant here. Whereas the roles of the sports player/coach and the sports club executive are utterly distinct, the trader's boss still benefits from the same false ideology of rare white-collar talent that secures an extremely large salary for himself, albeit not as large as the trader's.)

The institutional shareholder is susceptible to the same bias as the executive. When he approves the high salaries of the senior executives of a sports club or television company in which he invests, he is supporting the talent ideology from which he, and certainly the senior executives in his own company, will often profit. But he will have nothing to lose personally from countering the principle of high pay for sports stars and celebrities that are employed by the same organisation.

It is interesting to note, too, that much of the supporting cast surrounding high pay in the corporate world is absent from the arena of sports stars and celebrities. Pay consultants are hired to apply an additional layer of credibility, to issue specious justifications and to introduce superfluous complexity to obfuscate total compensation. These are not needed for sports stars and celebrities.

Meanwhile, the journalists and writers who regularly defend the scale of executive pay for the benefit of their readers in the corporate world – and for that matter, for the benefit of their interviewees, their sources for stories and their hosts for extremely enjoyable dinners and sporting events who also inhabit that world – are altogether quieter on the issue of high sports and celebrity pay, where elaborate justifications are both needless and clearly unrelated to any possible personal advantage. In these worlds, it's not necessary to fake it.

Who Are the Fakes?

"Faking it" was a popular and award-winning show on British television for several years, and its format was subsequently sold throughout the world. Each week, the show followed a volunteer from one walk of life who lives and trains with an expert from a completely different field. After a four-week crash course in their mentor's area of expertise, the volunteer was put to the test by competing against genuine practitioners. A panel of seasoned industry "experts" was then given the task of identifying which of the four participants was the faker.

The individual shows were given titles like "Burger Flipper to Chef" and "Kickboxer to Ballroom Dancer". Week after week, the fakers fooled the "experts". An emergency telephone line operator convinced as a TV director, a newsagent successfully faked it as a showbiz reporter, a punk rocker learned to read music and conducted an orchestra in such a professional manner that the panel was duped.

Answer this: if a fit, very tall, young man who played some basketball in his spare time was asked to play for the Los Angeles Lakers, do you think he would be more or less able to "fake it" once he stepped onto the basketball court, than would an intelligent, well-educated, 52-year-old white male asked to perform the role of a chief executive?

High pay for top-performing sports stars is rational, even if not always proved to have been the correct decision in retrospect. High pay for senior executives of successful large companies is at best a shot in the dark, and at worst, and in my view, an elaborately constructed theft, the results of which are hugely damaging to society as a whole.

If you are persuaded that this status quo is bad, the question then becomes a practical one: what now needs to be done to change it?

Restitution

In a Harvard Business Review article published in 2003, Roger Martin and Mihnea Moldoveanu trace capital's hard-fought and ultimately victorious twentieth-century conflict against organised labour.

In the new century, the authors argue, capital faces a potentially even more formidable enemy in this battle for control of the economy. That enemy is "talent". Modern-day companies "cannot generate profits without the ideas, skills, and talent of knowledge workers, and they have to bet on people." As this dependence on the perceived value of the alleged cream of the workforce has increased, so "talented" workers have been able to seize an ever greater share of the profits from shareholders.

This battle, say the authors, will only intensify: "As investments in people add more to a company's competitiveness relative to capital investments, companies cannot reward only their shareholders with capital gains. They will have to reward key employees, too."

The contemporary twist is that "capital" no longer constitutes a handful of phenomenally wealthy and powerful local barons. Nowadays, ownership is dispersed throughout the population. As Martin and Moldoveanu put it, "the largest shareholders are pension funds, which primarily invest the savings of the working class."

When you also count individual shareholdings, mutual funds and financial institutions and insurance companies that are themselves public companies, one can confidently say that the population at large owns the vast majority of the international stock market. In other words, the "talented" are rewarding themselves with money taken from the rest of the population.

The article certainly provides us with an invaluable framework for understanding the magnitude of the battle ahead, and the strength of the forces grouped on either side.

However, the perspective fails to see anything untoward in this massive shift in the balance of power towards the "talent class"; it is merely a fact worth observing, the result of the transition to a new type of economy.

In reality, the shift does not simply represent a natural and inevitable stage in a historical process, signifying the equitable distribution of reward for a dynamic modern era, with wealth now allocated to the supremely able ahead of the privileged. No-one can of course deny that meritocracy is more apparent in Western society as a whole than several decades ago, and that a greater, albeit still limited, number of opportunities exists for women, ethnic minorities and people from the developing world and poorer backgrounds. But in the world of large corporations, meritocracy is all too often just a convenient smokescreen.

Here, the "talent class" has been predominantly hijacked by those whose abilities are unexceptional, and its supporting ideology, so neatly summarised by the authors, has been shamelessly abused in order to justify the wrongful expropriation of enormous wealth from the mass of the working population.

In using ideology to cement their personal position, corporate executives actually behave in an entirely predictable manner, following in a similar tradition to other groups who have found themselves in the ascendancy and wanted to keep it that way.

During the Soviet era, for example, the "nomenklatura" class of apparatchiks parroted the gospel of Marxism-Leninism, not least as a means of preserving their own status and resulting privilege. Just like the talent ideology, Communist doctrine designated an exclusive vanguard of exceptional people to play the "leading role". It is interesting to note, too, that convoluted jargon, a sure sign of self-serving dishonesty and dissembling, has also been common to both Soviet communism and the corporate world.

The first and by far the most important stage in the process of restitution, of people reclaiming what is rightfully theirs, has to be the fundamental reappraisal, even dismantling of the talent ideology. Only then can capital reassert itself in its battle against this adulterated "talent class". Only then can entrepreneurship become the accepted route to attaining great personal wealth in business. Only then can we progress to a new and yet more productive era.

The Pack of Cards

No-one should be under any illusions about the extent and nature of the fight ahead. Those who owe their wealth to the talent ideology will fight tooth and nail to defend its tenets. The finance industry, as a whole, will be particularly defiant.

Many of those who feed off the "talent" class (the pay consultants, the headhunters, the business schools and other constituencies) will be similarly energised. And the ambitious lower down the corporate hierarchy will reject any assault on the ideology that burnishes their self-image as they climb the ladder, and which promises to vest them with untold riches if and when they reach the top.

There are plenty, too, who benefit directly from the ideology without earning millions, and who will also defend their corner resolutely. Executives in the state sector, heads of medium-sized companies, senior editors and executives of newspapers and television companies who control the prism through which we view this issue, are among those who have much to protect.

Just like their better-paid counterparts at the top of public companies and throughout the finance sector, they often receive pay completely out of kilter with a rational interpretation of the true realities of supply and demand, not to mention high status and the admiration of their peers. Intelligent, competent and hard-working they may all be, but the talent ideology disguises the fact that many other intelligent, competent and hard-working people would have equal chance of doing their jobs equally well.

Nor should we discount the resistance of the institutional shareholders who are meant to act on our behalf, and whose workers, especially in leadership positions, profit from the self-same ideology.

But the strength and will of the opposition should not intimidate us into meek acquiescence. We want our money back! If they defend their income on the basis of their superior talent – or, more ridiculously, on the basis that they are comparable to sports or film stars – we should insistently demand convincing justification for such claims. It is up to them to persuade us, the ultimate shareholders, why we should pay them so much money.

Executive pay has not increased so much in the last thirty years only because of self-interest. As ownership has become increasingly dispersed, the ultimate shareholders have also provided desultory opposition, a weakness that has been ruthlessly exploited. It is not enough to grumble about high pay; free societies do not change without the dedication and persistence of large numbers of people. Shareholder activism – that's you and I – is key to combating vested interests, and instigating progress.

Free-market capitalism is still under construction. Emerging as the dominant economic system within what is now the developed world only in the nineteenth century, and in much of the developing world only in the past three decades, the culture surrounding it is in its infancy and evolving rapidly. There is nothing automatic about high pay for senior executives; and once the talent ideology has been thoroughly confronted, and people are armed with the necessary arguments and properly organised and mobilised to fight the fight, executive pay should return to rational and justifiable levels.

Missing the Point

But how exactly should high pay be reformed? Since the crisis of 2008, experts and governments have been immersed in heated debate about how to remodel the pay of finance workers, so that they don't endanger the stability of our entire economic system in pursuit of huge short-term, personal reward.

The issue has been right at the forefront of the international political agenda. In September 2009, news coverage of the G20 conference of leaders of the world's largest economies was dominated by the debate about bank bonuses. Some Western leaders become unusually animated over bankers' pay, often using very unleaderlike language. German Chancellor Angela Merkel noted that bonus payments "quite rightly drives a lot of people up the wall", while Nicolas Sarkozy, the French President, labeled them a "scandal".

However, cultural and political differences, largely between the United States and mainland Europe, appear likely to obstruct meaningful international reform. So far, the most far-reaching G20 proposal is a framework, to be implemented by each country's regulator, whereby multi-year guaranteed pay deals are banned and bonus deals deferred over a number of years, or even "clawed back" if a big deal subsequently sours. The organisation also urged national regulators to limit total compensation as a percentage of total net revenue for under-capitalised banks, but did not specify what this limit should be.

The proposals put forward throughout the world may all be

thoughtful, detailed and well-meaning. But the mainstream debate misses the one crucial point: while the technical experts produce elaborate plans on exactly how huge wealth should be awarded, they neglect to ask whether it should be awarded at all.

There is no rational reason why top finance workers should be paid any more than top workers in the advertising industry, or in the pharmaceutical industry, or in the computer industry, or in any industry in the knowledge economy for that matter. Investment banking may generate huge revenue, but that revenue belongs to the shareholders.

Should the workers themselves get paid more money just because they deal with money as a commodity? Nobody seems to be suggesting that cashiers in high street banks get paid large amounts of money because they handle it all day, or that successful shoe salesmen get given a mountain of shoes.

Similar proposals are regularly put forward with respect to senior executives in all public companies. Again, the experts tackle the detail of pay awards, with the intention of best aligning their interests with those of the shareholders, but ignore the fundamental problem with the irrational level of their overall compensation.

They ask: How do we motivate these executives properly if we reduce their pay? You might just as well ask : how on earth have we managed to motivate hard-working but much lower-paid people in many different pursuits, including the hard-working and much lower-paid chief executives of yesteryear?

Unhealthy State

At the same time, there are risks of misfiring or hitting the wrong targets. There have been calls from some commentators, and moves from certain European governments, to introduce legally enforceable caps on bonuses or even bans on bonuses per se. Others talk of extremely high levels of taxation aimed at the most handsomely rewarded bankers. Such government intervention would be, for a variety of reasons, futile and even self-defeating.

First, highly-paid corporate workers, and their army of pay consultants and international tax lawyers, will doubtless find a way round the system to protect the real level of their compensation against governmental, or even regulatory, interference.

Since late 2008, we have seen bailed-out banks greatly increase the level of basic salaries offered to their top staff to offset the reduction in bonuses necessary to placate public opinion and the authorities. If formal and blanket bonus bans or caps are introduced, we may also witness a large increase in benefits-in-kind, where employers offer help with such expenditure as housing and fees for their children's education.

And if such caps are introduced in one country rather than internationally, then banks might simply relocate in order to preserve the personal wealth of their top employees. "If we said we're not going to have as big bonuses or the same bonuses as last year," said Lord Griffiths, vice-chairman of Goldman Sachs International, to a London audience in October 2009, "I think then you'd find that lots of City firms could easily hive off their operations to Switzerland or the far east." Whatever might one think of a board member of a major public company holding an entire country to ransom by threatening to deny it huge corporate tax revenue, it is clear that exclusively domestic remedies will fail.

If the G20's proposal to limit the share of revenue that under-capitalised banks can spend on total compensation is implemented, then ways will simply be found to reduce the money allotted to ordinary workers in an attempt to maintain the bonuses of the "talented".

Second, punitive taxation is extremely unlikely to be directed with specific accuracy at the very top earners in the corporate world. Wealth-creating entrepreneurs, including those in the finance sector, will also undeservedly suffer, as will high earners in the worlds of sport and entertainment. Why should they?

Third, even if such taxation were only targeted at the corporate world, it would likely be set at such a level that it would penalise those deserving earners, such as top sales people in the non-finance sector, whose pay is more rational and less artificially inflated by the talent ideology. There may even be certain instances in the finance sector where very high pay is more rational, such as the mathematical experts who devise financial products (although whether such a breed can now be considered particularly desirable post-crisis, or even rare given the number of gifted Maths graduates in the emerging world, is open to question).

Flooding the Pipeline

The glamour of finance resides less in the nature of the work, than in the pay cheques that are justified by the myth of rare talent. Puncture the talent ideology, the pay will subside, and the glamour will dissipate.

Simple in theory, but there may be complications in practice. We can expect a glut of suitable candidates to want the lower-paid but still high-status senior executive positions in public companies. But who will want to remain in the much lower-paid, unglamorous finance sector, in positions in the hierarchy that boast only moderate social status?

We also have the accompanying problem of short-term replaceability. If we drastically reduce pay within public companies in the finance sector too suddenly, employees may leave in droves, a short-term risk that responsible managers would generally not take. Here a phased reduction in pay, together with temporary over-employment at a lower level, may work.

Companies could recruit plenty of fresh graduates and people with a modicum of experience in other sectors, and then train them intensively on the job and through formal business education. As the transition period continues, an increasing number of able people should be in a position to take up the reins if and when people leave. This might help to reset salary expectations and trigger a deflationary spiral.

As well as a huge reduction in the proportion of revenue allotted to employee salaries in finance companies, pooled bonuses ought to become more commonplace, with an identical percentage of salary awarded to each employee in a team or department. It will always be extremely difficult to measure the impact of one employee, particularly in a large company. While it may still also be tough to measure the precise impact of a complete team, when set against competing external factors such as a booming economy, it is certainly less so.

Opening Up

How can the pay of senior executives throughout the corporate world be reduced? Demanding greater transparency and accountability has to be the first step.

Perhaps companies ought to publish the earnings ratio between their highest-paid and lowest-paid full-time worker in their accounts. Grass-roots employees and/or shareholders will benefit from a low ratio, particularly when business is good. Unless demonstrably justifiable, a very high ratio can be castigated as a gross abdication of corporate social responsibility, reflecting very negatively on the external public image that companies claim to care so deeply about. Excessive pay is bad for society – the truly socially responsible seek to reduce it.

Annual shareholder elections for remuneration committees that decide on executive pay would be advisable, so that they constantly have to justify pay levels. And we should not be fooled by small percentage increases, supposedly indicating greater restraint. A small percentage increase on far too much still equals far too much. Substantial decreases are imperative.

As for precisely what their salary should be, no-one is suggesting that they ought to receive the same as the average worker. The skills that they require will certainly be less common and, therefore, less replaceable; it's just that they are by no means very uncommon, or irreplaceable.

In 1961, the organisational psychologist Elliott Jaques set out his concept of "felt-fair pay". He concluded from his research that people throughout an organisation, whatever their level in the hierarchy, had a very similar sense of what each level deserves to earn. The recipient's "felt-fair pay" equates to this consensus figure.

By the early 1980s, Jaques had declared that the CEO of a major corporation has a "felt-fair pay" 96 times greater than that of those in the grass-roots of the company who perform daily routine tasks. It hardly needs repeating that the reality today is quite different. The average total earnings for a large company CEO in the United States in 2008 was $10.8 million, making the relevant multiple somewhere between 300-400.

Bidding Down

But rather than attempting to specify exactly what a CEO deserves to earn, a course which appears to me to be wide open to abuse from the purveyors of the talent ideology, perhaps we should approach the issue from a completely different angle. Namely, how little can we get an appropriate candidate to do the job for?

I have argued that there are a significant number of people who have the ability to be a CEO of a major company. I would also argue that a large proportion of these people would still be delighted to be offered the role even at a significantly reduced salary.

After all, there are many non-financial attractions of the job, not least the status involved. You would certainly stand to make quite an impression at a dinner party if, in answer to the obligatory question from a newly-made acquaintance about your occupation, you could reply "chief executive of Goldman Sachs, actually".

The President of the United States earns $400,000, the President of the World Bank earns less ($391,440) and the President of France earns less still at €240,000 (or $336,000). But there appears no shortage of ambitious presidents-in-waiting out there.

Why? Because these aspirants are not so much motivated by money as they are by power, prestige and potential impact. We can reasonably conclude that similar motivations would encourage a host of excellent candidates to apply for the role of chief executive of a major company, even if salaries were reduced to the paltry level of our presidents, and would also ensure that executives perform to their utmost in order to reap the resulting acclaim.

You could say that the world of politics is very different from the world of business, where money and profits are, rightly, the overriding goal. And in relation to privately-owned or small companies, you would be completely correct.

But just like our political leaders or even senior civil servants, chief executives of large public companies are performing a public duty, in their case by serving the interests of the shareholders, i.e. the population at large. They should not be placed on a pedestal above us, their fellow citizens; they have been invited to represent the people, and should derive honour and pride from this invitation. The idea that public servants should also seek to be paid millions appears distasteful.

Indeed, the head of the largest bank in the world, Jiang Jianqing of the Industrial and Commercial Bank of China, earned just $234,700 in 2008, a figure earned by his US counterparts in a matter of a few days. Despite what his comparatively low salary might indicate to some, Jianqing was sufficiently "talented" and "motivated" to lead his company to a profit of more than $16 billion in that year, the same year so many Western banks needed their governments to save them from bankruptcy.

All these factors – the number of suitable candidates, the non-financial incentives, the public responsibility – should exert downward pressure on chief executive pay. When all the willing candidates have been sifted through, shareholders should ask those shortlisted to specify the lowest salary, and bonus incentives, they would accept. The candidate with the lowest bid gets the job. At the very least the bidding should act as a criterion for decision-making, just like it would be in any transparent public tender.

A Departing Act

Earlier, we saw Neville Isdell, the former Coca-Cola chief executive, proclaiming that "successful succession", finding someone to replace him, would be his "most important" achievement. Indeed, "succession planning" is currently a very fashionable concept among executives and their consultants. What about offering one last bonus incentive to current chief executives to encourage them to find an appropriate successor for a fraction of their own pay, and thus break the cycle of excessive reward? In this way, much-vaunted "succession planning" might replace the current "procession planning", and for once serve the shareholder.

Large companies have a duty to their shareholders to save costs by "commoditising" the skills of their employees. This is achieved through instituting an efficient and self-perpetuating business operation within which no one employee is indispensable.

With the bulk of the workforce, they have certainly fulfilled this responsibility. In other words, the vast majority of employees are regarded as very replaceable; their labour is viewed as a commodity and is thus relatively cheap. With the aid of the talent ideology, however, top executives have promulgated the myth that their own labour is not a commodity. We should perhaps incentivise this last batch of highly-paid CEOs to do what they have so far scandalously failed to do - commoditise themselves.

At the same time, it might also be a good idea to set a floor beyond below which the total CEO compensation level cannot fall, to stop the application process being usurped by the independently wealthy and to limit the risk of corruption. The pay of the political leader of the country in which the company is based would seem a reasonable lower limit, and would reinforce the notion of public service.

If there are ten rungs in a standard large corporate hierarchy in the United States, and if the lowest rung pays $40,000 with each step up the ladder involving a very considerable and motivating 30 per cent increase, then we will arrive very near the relevant figure of $400,000 anyway. Why should those towards the top get such a gargantuan percentage raise?

This greatly reduced pay should, in turn, help to realign the salaries of the senior executive team, who also occupy high-status positions with great public responsibility, and who naturally compare their income with the CEO's. In this new system, there may well be a few valuable individuals with rare ability making a measurable and substantial positive impact lower down the hierarchy who will earn more than the top tier.

The pay of certain high positions in the state sector should also fall in response, with the usual justification regarding the need to compete with the stratospheric salaries of "talented" top executives in the business world no longer so relevant. In this way, the taxpayer and the shareholder, incidentally the same person, both win.

Furthermore, re-imagining top executives as public servants should serve to deglamourize the climb up the corporate ladder. Senior employees in large companies may operate in the commercial sphere, dealing in large sums of money and making important strategic decisions. But at the end of the day, they are not actually businesspeople. They are what they are – employees. They have not set up on their own and taken a risk, like the businessperson who runs a local restaurant or hair salon.

If the young and ambitious aspire to be considered as cut-and-thrust dynamic businesspeople, not as highly competent public servants, employees or functionaries, they must first leave the world of large corporations behind.

They must enter instead a completely different world – one where individuals stand on their own two feet, this time unsupported by a heavyweight brand and infrastructure they played no part in establishing; where wealth is attainable through ingenuity and relentless dedication, not as a corollary of occupying the highest rungs of a ladder that numerous other, very similar people, might just as easily occupy.

To become rich in business, you should need to do it yourself. A tough call, but if you're really that good, if you really are a talented star, it shouldn't be impossible. "I enjoy a challenge" is what people are taught to say before an interview. Why not take on a real one instead, and become an entrepreneur?

Winning the War against Talent

In 1979, the eminent economist John Kenneth Galbraith pondered executive pay in his book "Annals of an Abiding Liberal":

"As an individual rises in this hierarchy, his bureaucratic power increases – and among the things so increased is the power to set his own compensation. Thus compensation in the large corporation has become very generous. No-one can seriously pretend (although some do) that it depends on the scarcity, and thus the market price, of the talent involved." And he adds: "The salary of the chief executive of the large corporation is not a market reward for achievement. It is frequently in the nature of a warm personal gesture by the individual to himself. This no-one likes to say."

Thirty years on, much water has passed under the bridge. Nowadays, people can't stop pretending about scarce talent, and senior executive and finance sector pay is no longer merely a self-awarded warm personal gesture, meriting no more than an amusing put-down; it is now a self-awarded passport to extreme wealth, brazenly seized from the pockets of ordinary people, and built on the foundations of a disingenuous, self-interested and ultimately shallow ideology.

The newly-formed "talent class" now stands astride the great system of capitalism, mocking its fundamental precepts, deflating its energy and milking it for undeserved personal gain. The possible dire consequences of this supremacy range from the gradual erosion of popular credibility in the economic system, right through to sudden and disastrous self-combustion.

But the battle against high pay will not be won through capricious anger, or through half-hearted tinkering at the edges. Nor will it be won through stale arguments about greed and inequality. But through popular commitment and rational and persistent argument, the impostors will retreat, and sense will prevail.

ENDNOTES

Chapter 1: The Poison Carrot

Page 1

Bob Diamond 2007 pay: The Times, 27 March 2008

Ray Irani 2006 pay: Los Angeles Times, 7 April 2007

Top soccer players in Europe, such as Lionel Messi and Cristiano Ronaldo, can earn upwards of $200,000 per week.

Page 2

Peston, R., "Barclays Diamond Geezer", BBC Website, 26 March 2007

Page 5
For the comparison between average CEO pay and average blue-collar pay in the United States, see research by The American Federation of Labor and Congress of Industrial Organizations (AFL-CIO), 2005

For the average proportion of profits paid to the top five executives in US public companies, see Bebchuk, L. and Grinstein, Y. (2005) "The Growth of Executive Pay", Oxford Review of Economic Policy, Vol.21, No.2

Page 7

For the proportion of newly named CEOs appointed from inside the company in 2007, see www.webershandwick.com

Page 10

Richard Fuld 2006 and 2007 pay: Financial Times, 22 December 2008

Page 13

For the realities of entrepreneurship, see Shane, S., "The Illusions of Entrepreneurship: The Costly Myths that Entrepreneurs, Investors and Policy Makers Live By" (Yale University Press, 2008)

Page 14

Lazear, E. and Rosen, S. (1981) "Rank-order tournaments as optimum labor contracts", Journal of Political Economy, October

Page 15

City of London 2007 bonuses: Reuters, 7 October 2007

JP Morgan and Goldman Sachs 2008 bonuses: The Times, 31 July 2009

Page 16

For underperformance caused by low expectations, see Pfeffer, J. (2001) "Fighting the war for talent is hazardous to your organization's health", Organizational Dynamics, Spring

Page 17

For an estimate of individual direct or indirect stock ownership throughout the world, see Grout, P., Megginson, W. and Zalewska, A. (2009) "One half-billion shareholders and counting – Determinants of individual share ownership around the world", Working Paper for Journal of Economic Literature

Jeffrey Immelt CNBC interview: www.finfacts.ie, 20 January 2007

Jeffrey Immelt 2007 pay: New York Times, 4 March 2008

Page 18

UK local government 2007/8 chief executive pay: The Guardian, 6 April 2009

Chapter 2: The Talent Ideology

Page 19

Vikram Pandit 2008 pay: www.equilar.com

Page 21

Drucker, P., "Landmarks of Tomorrow: A Report on the New 'Post-Modern' World" (Harper & Brothers, 1959)

For an estimate of the number of knowledge workers in the United States, see Lowell, B. (2004) "Making a Market in Knowledge", McKinsey Quarterly, No. 3

According to pwc.com, PwC revenue for 2008 was $28.2 billion. The 2008 number of employees is quoted by www.hoovers.com.

Page 23

For the McKinsey article, see Chambers, E. et al (1998) "The War for Talent", McKinsey Quarterly, No.3

Page 28

For the book on the same subject, see Michaels, E., Handfield-Jones, H. and Axelrod, B. (2001) "The War for Talent", Harvard Business School Press

Gladwell, M., "The Talent Myth", The New Yorker, 22 July 2002

For the significance of emotional development, see Higgs, M. and Dulewitz, V. (1999) "Making Sense of Emotional Intelligence" or Goleman, D. (1999) "Working with emotional intelligence"

Page 29

For details on the 25 wealthiest entrepreneurs in the UK in 2007, see The Times, 3 July 2007

Page 33

Kay, I. and van Putten, S., "The Myths and Realities of Executive Pay" (Cambridge University Press, 2007), p.12

Page 34

For statistics on female representation on company boards, see 2008 Catalyst Census of Women Board Directors of the Fortune 500 and www.the-chiefexecutive.com, 9 October 2008

For Malcolm Gladwell's survey on the proportion of tall men among American CEOs, see excerpt from his book "Blink" on www.gladwell.com

Page 35

For an estimate of the annual number of science and engineering graduates in China and India, see The Economist, 16 September 2006

Page 36

For the survey of human resources professionals, see article to mark tenth anniversary of the original War for Talent research: Guthridge, M., Komm, A., Lawson E. (2008) "Making Talent a Strategic Priority", McKinsey Quarterly, No.1

Walker, M. (2009) "The World's New Numbers",
The Wilson Quarterly, Spring

Page 37

Development Dimensions International, in co-operation with the Economist Intelligence Unit (2008) "Growing Global Executive Talent"

Chapter 3: Neglected Terrain

Page 43

Rynecki, D., "Putting the Muscle Back Into the Bull", Fortune, 5 April 2004

Stan O'Neal 2003 pay: Fortune, 5 April 2004; 2004 pay: USA Today, 30 March 2005; 2005 pay: AP Online, 3 October 2006; 2006 pay: www.msnbc.com, 19 March 2007

Page 44

Stan O'Neal payout: Bloomberg, 2 November 2007

Lewis, M., "O'Neal's Agony, or, in the Bunker with Stan", Bloomberg, 6 November 2007

Cramer, J., "Street Justice", New York Magazine, 12 November 2007

For the poll on the worst CEOs of all time, see www.portfolio.com, 22 April 2009

Page 45

Rosenzweig, P., "An obstacle to evidence-based management: the halo effect", www.evidence-basedmanagement.com, 5 February 2007

Page 46

Miller, S., "Interview with Phil Rosenzweig", www.b-eye-network.co.uk, 31 July 2007

Page 47

Goldman Sachs projected 2009 pay: Bloomberg, 14 July 2009; BBC News website, 14 July 2009; Daily Telegraph, 2 July 2009

Page 48

For statistics on global investment banking revenue, see International Financial Services London report, "Banking 2008", February 2008 and International Financial Services London report, "International Financial Markets in the UK", May 2009

Percentage of investment banking revenue going to employees: The New York Times, 26 April 2009

Percentage of revenue from "Big Four" American team sports going to employees: SportsBusiness Journal, 15 December 2008

Percentage of revenue from top soccer clubs going to employees: Deloitte Annual Review of Football Finance 2009

Percentage of 2008 Morgan Stanley revenue going to employees: New York Times, 26 April 2009

Page 50

Tony Hayward 2008 pay: Dow Jones Newswires, 7 April 2009

Jeroen van der Veer 2008 pay: The Times, 6 May 2009

Page 51

One paper from 2001 claimed to demonstrate that chief executives have greater influence on company performance in certain industries than in others (see Wasserman, N., Nohria, N. and Anand, B. (2001) "When does leadership matter? The contingent opportunities view of CEO leadership" Harvard Business School Working Paper, April). But to go along with this finding, we have to assume that it was the CEO who was responsible for the difference in performance, rather than a whole host of other factors. And even if we accept this huge assumption, there is little reason to think that many other virtually identical people, in the same position, would not have had a similar effect.

Page 52

For top companies' capitalisation and number of employees, see FT Global 500 2009, Financial Times, 29 May 2009

Page 53

James McNerney 2008 pay: www.equilar.com

Tom Glocer 2008 pay: Financial Post, 30 March 2009

Daniel Glaser 2008 pay: www.forbes.com

Greg Case 2008 pay: www.businessweek.com

Page 54

For projections on omega-3 sales, see "Omega 3 fatty acids and the U.S. Food and Beverage Market", Packaged Facts, 1 March, 2007

Page 55

Jean-Pierre Garnier 2008 pay and annual pension: The Guardian, 5 March 2009

Page 56

Neville Isdell 2005 pay: Business Week, 17 April 2007; 2006 and 2007 pay: Reuters, 3 March 2008

Page 57

For Isdell's comments on succession, see Collier, J., "Isdell passes his last baton at Coca-Cola", The Atlanta Journal-Constitution, 26 April 2009

Millward Brown 2009 report,
"The Top 100 Most Valuable Global Brands"

Page 58

Neville Isdell annual pension: www.aflcio.org, "CEO Golden Years:
The 25 Largest CEO Pensions", compiled by the AFL-CIO and The
Corporate Library

Page 59

Walton, M and Deming, W. Edwards "The Deming management
method", p.88

Drucker, P., "The Concept of the Corporation" (Transaction Publishers,
1993), p.33

Page 61

For Marcus Buckingham research on engagement, see Labarre, P. (2001)
"Marcus Buckingham thinks your boss has an attitude problem",
Fast Company, August

Page 62

Tatchell, N. and Crawley, J. (2007) "Towers Perrin Global Workforce
Study", www.eiu.com, 13 November

Rosenzweig, P., "The Halo Effect" (Free Press, 2007), p.142

Page 63

Sy,T., Coté, S. and Saavedra, R. (2005) "The Contagious Leader: Impact
of the Leader's Mood on the Mood of Group Members, Group Affective
Tone, and Group Processes", Journal of Applied Psychology, No.90

Chapter 4: The Gravy Train Engine

Page 69

For the multiple of CEO pay to average worker pay, see joint Institute for Policy Studies and United for a Fair Economy report, "Executive Excess 2007: The Staggering Social Cost of US Business Leadership", 29 August 2007

President of the United States pay: www.businessweek.com, 11 February 2009

Page 70

Kay, I. and van Putten, S., "The Myths and Realities of Executive Pay" (Cambridge University Press, 2007), p.19

Page 73

For average grocery supermarket revenue, see First Research report, "Grocery Stores and Supermarkets", March 2008

For percentage of turnover in England soccer clubs spent on salaries, see Dobson, S. and Goddard, J., "The Economics of Football" (Cambridge University Press, 2001), p.93 and Deloitte Annual Review of Football Finance 2009

Page 75

Peters, T., "The Pursuit of WOW!" (Random House, 1994), p.36

Page 78

Hayes, M. and Schaefer, S. (2009) "CEO Pay and the Lake Wobegon Effect", Journal of Financial Economics, Forthcoming

Page 79

Wighton, D., "More than money at risk for Goldman Sachs bosses", The Times, 15 July 2009

Page 80

Sir Fred Goodwin agreed in June 2009 to reduce his annual pension from £703,000 ($1.12 million) to £342,500 ($582,000). However, he also received a £2.7 million ($4.6 million) lump sum in exchange for the reduction on his annual payments. See The Wall Street Journal, 19 June 2009

For an example of literature explaining why it is very useful to fail, see Maxwell, J., "Failing Forward" (Thomas Nelson, 2000)

Page 81

Wendelin Wiedeking 2008 pay and payoff: www.ft.com, 23 July 2009

Bob Nardelli pay for six years as CEO of Home Depot: The Times, 6 August 2007

Richard Fuld total pay as Lehman Brothers CEO: www.equilar.com

For details on Richard Fuld's hearing at The House Committee on Oversight and Government Reform, see Moore, H. "Congress Grills Lehman Brothers's Dick Fuld", Wall Street Journal Blogs, 6 October 2008

Page 83

Snyder, M., "Why city fat cats deserve their pay – and our respect", The Observer, 16 September 2007

For comparative statistics on job risk for a large company CEO and the average worker, see See Isles, N. (2007) "The Risk Myth: CEOs and Labour Market Risk", The Work Foundation Provocation Series

Page 84

Bob Nardelli annual pension: www.aflcio.org, "CEO Golden Years: The 25 Largest CEO Pensions", compiled by the AFL-CIO and The Corporate Library

Dixon, H., "Walker's pay proposals don't hit mark", www.breakingviews.com, 16 July 2009

United States Department of Labor, "Occupational Outlook Handbook", 2008-9 edition

Page 85

Citrin, J. (2009) "So...do you still want to be a CEO?", The Conference Board Review, May/June

Chapter 5: Fame and Fortune

Page 90

Bebchuk, L. and Fried, J., "Pay without Performance: The Unfulfilled Promise of Executive Compensation" (Harvard University Press, 2004), p.21

Page 91

Maria Sharapova 2007-8 earnings: www.forbes.com, 22 July 2008

Sharapova's earnings were $26 million during this period. The Associated Press (2 May 2009) compiled a list of the top ten highest-paid CEOs in Standard & Poor's 500 companies for 2008, the year of the worst financial crisis since the 1930s Depression. Number ten was Harvard graduate Jamie Dimon of JP Morgan Chase, a bank that received $25 billion of US government bailout assistance in the same year. Dimon's total compensation was $35.7 million.

Angelina Jolie 2008-9 pay: www.forbes.com, 1 July 2009

Page 92

Mahendra Singh Dhoni 2008-9 earnings: www.forbes.com, 27 August 2009

Major League Lacrosse approximate player pay: www.lacrosseforums.com

Page 93

Estimated Larry Lloyd pay in 1970s: In autobiographies of top soccer players from that era, a weekly wage of £250 to £300 is often quoted.

Somehow one can't imagine two-time European Cup winners like Ryan Giggs selling his medals in future life. Giggs started his professional career with Manchester United in 1991, and after 18 years at the top, is still estimated to earn a basic annual salary of around £4 million ($6.8 million) in 2009 (The Daily Telegraph, 6 February 2009)

Page 94

According to the official website of the Irish Football Association (www.irishfa.com), George Best's career at international level never matched the highs of his time at Manchester United, though there were highlights such as his superlative display against the Scots at Windsor Park in 1967 when he single-handedly destroyed the opposition with a performance of breathtaking skill.

Page 95

For an analysis of the portability of American footballer skills, see Groysberg, B., Sant, L. and Abrahams, R. (2008) "When Stars Migrate, Do They Still Perform Like Stars?", MIT Sloan Management Review, Fall

Alex Rodriguez pay at New York Yankees: www.espn.com, 13 December 2007

Alex Rodriguez pay at Texas Rangers: www.mlb.com, 13 December 2007

Page 97

The academic literature on the merits of hiring an industry outsider as a chief executive is extremely complex, quite contradictory and, as a body of research, offers no definitive conclusions. For discussion of the possible merits, see for example, Karaevli, A. (2007) "Performance Consequences of New CEO "Outsiderness": Moderating Effects of Pre- and Post-Succession Contexts", Strategic Management Journal, July; and Bailey, E. and Helfat, C. (2003). "External management succession, human capital, and firm performance: an integrative analysis," Managerial and Decision Economics, No.4

Page 98

The respective roles of luck and skill in market trading are keenly debated. No-one, however, seriously disputes that the random hand of chance does play a major role. Even when an investment manager outperforms the market over a considerable period of time, we can't discount the possibility that their success was lucky. By the law of probabilities, there will be a small number within a very large sample which may win continually in a random game. In a sports game, on the other hand, the playing team is more or less solely responsible for its own destiny in its battle with opponents. For one example of random stock picks outperforming investment professionals over a given period, see Liang, Y. Ramchander, S. and Sharma, J. (1995) "The Performance of Stocks: Professional versus Dartboard Picks", Journal of Financial and Strategic Decisions, Spring

Page 100

Phil Jackson 2009 pay: www.forbes.com, 13 May 2009

Kobe Bryant 2009 pay: www.espn.com, 1 July 2009

Terry Francona pay: www.espn.com, 25 February 2008

Boston Red Sox players' pay: www.foxsports.com

Lionel Messi pay: www.reuters.com, 18 September 2009

Pep Guardiola 2009 pay: www.goal.com, 19 March 2009

Page 101

For details on Gallup survey, see Buckingham, M. and Coffman, C., "First, Break All the Rules: What the World's Greatest Managers Do Differently" (Simon & Schuster, 2001), p.11

As one of many examples of player loyalty to coaches, the former soccer player Viv Anderson says of Brian Clough, his coach at Nottingham Forest who led the provincial club to a remarkable two European Cups: "As a manager you would run through a brick wall for him because he had something about him." (www.skysports.com, 13 April 2009)

Page 102

Luis Felipe Scolari, the then Chelsea coach, had a very modest playing career in Brazil. Arsenal's Arsène Wenger and Liverpool's Rafael Benitez had similarly unimpressive playing records in France and Spain respectively. Manchester United's Alex Ferguson was by some distance the best player of the quartet, but never represented Scotland in a senior international match

Page 103

Average 2008 large company CEO pay in United States: The New York Times, 4 April 2009

According to a YouGov poll in the UK in August 2009, 93 per cent believed soccer players were overpaid, compared to 74 per cent for bankers and 80 per cent for TV stars (see www.guardian.co.uk, 28 August 2009)

Page 104

Katie Couric annual pay at CBS: Wall Street Journal, 10 April 2008

Katie Couric annual pay at NBC: New York Times, 20 December 2001

After a promising first week with Couric as anchor, "CBS Evening News" then fell back, repeatedly placed third nationally in the race with ABC and NBC. Ratings later increased during and after the screening of Couric's highly-regarded interview with vice-presidential candidate Sarah Palin, and showed further signs of recovery in 2009

Page 105

Adler, M. (1985) "Stardom and Talent", American Economic Review, March

David Beckham contract details at LA Galaxy: BBC website, 12 January 2007

For analysis of the influence of celebrity on sports stars' pay, see Lucifora, C. and Simmons, R. (2003) "Superstar effects in sport: Evidence from Italian soccer" Journal of Sports Economics, No.4, and Garcia-del-Barrio, P. and Pujol, F. (2007) "Hidden monopsony rents in winner-take-all markets – sport and economic contribution of Spanish soccer players", Managerial and Decision Economics, January

Page 108

David Gill 2008 pay: The Guardian, 29 October 2008

Wayne Rooney annual pay: Daily Mail, 31 May 2009

Conclusion: Restitution

Page 111

Martin, R. and Moldoveanu, M. (2003) "Capital Versus Talent", Harvard Business Review, July

Page 112

For a breakdown of the proportion of stock owned by various interests, see, for example, Federation of European Securities Exchanges Report (2008) "Share Ownership Structure in Europe"

Page 115

For some insightful contributions to the debate on reforming high bankers' pay, see Bebchuk, L. and Spamann, H. (2009) "Regulating Bankers' Pay", Harvard Law and Economics Discussion Paper, and Brown, P. and Thomas, H. (2009) "The Balanced Incentive Scheme", Policy Exchange

Page 120

Jaques, E., "Equitable Payment" (Heinemann, 1961)

Kleiner, A. (2001) "Elliot Jaques Levels With You",
Strategy + Business, No.1

President of World Bank annual pay: World Bank Annual Report, 2006

President of France annual pay: Reuters, 31 October 2007

Page 121

Jiang Jianqing 2008 pay: Reuters, 23 September 2009

Page 124

Galbraith, JK., "Annals of an Abiding Liberal" (Andre Deutsch, 1980), p.78-9

Acknowledgements

I would like to thank several people for helping me to write this book. Robin Shepherd and my wife, Janie, read through each chapter as the book progressed, and were always on hand to offer helpful thoughts and comments. David Taylor and Will Rosen read the completed draft, and provided invaluable overviews. Others, too numerous to mention, have helped me to crystallise my thoughts on high pay, not least the many commentators who take a very different line to my own.

I would also like to thank Steve Ward at Trim & Bleed for the cover and layout design, Elliot Wilson for his creative input and Jeff Scott, Jo Rosenfelder, Mark Phillips and Greg Allon for their expert advice on non-editorial matters.

Finally, I have once again to say a huge thank you to Janie, who has continued to be a fantastic source of support and encouragement to me throughout the draining and very lonely process of writing this book. With much love, I dedicate this book to her, and to our two beautiful children, Yael and Joe.

Author's Note

The exact figures for pay received by top executives mentioned in the book do vary according to the specific source consulted. As I explain at the beginning of Chapter 5, the opaqueness of executive pay is, in my view, quite deliberate. In the endnotes, I have detailed each source for the information I have used. Some may quibble with the figures quoted, but according to the logic of this book, it doesn't matter anyway. $15 million, $20 million, $25 million – it's too high, whatever it is.

I have used US dollars as the main currency as it is the most known internationally. The exchange rates I have used are the approximate averages since the beginning of 2006: €1 = $1.4 and £1 = $1.7.

I have used the pronoun "he" when referring to hypothetical corporate executives and finance workers. I make no apologies for this. As I noted in Chapter 2, almost all chief executives of major companies are men, and highly paid roles in the finance industry are also heavily dominated by men. I have written about the reasons for this elsewhere. The hypothetical entrepreneur in Chapter 1 is a "she", as this is a route to success that is open to all.

If any reader has a question to ask or a comment to make, they should feel free to contact me via my website www.davidbolchover.com. I shall try to respond to everyone.

INDEX

Lightning Source UK Ltd.
Milton Keynes UK
01 August 2010
157703UK00002B/2/P